Naked,
bare your soul

Naked, bare your soul

Published by Prospering Soul Publishing 14455 Gannet Street| Corona, CA |92880 www.aprosperingsoul.com

Prospering Soul Publishing is totally committed to publishing works that edify and exhort enabling the reader to prosper in their soul as III John 2 states.

Copyright 2015 by Jo Ann Carter for Karin Griffin

Cover design and page 153 photo by: Phoenix White of Emkrom Studios. Layout Design by: Kim Lewis of Creative By Design.

No part of this publication may be reproduced, stored in a retrieval system or transmitted in any way by any means, electronic, mechanical, photocopy, recording or otherwise without prior permission of the author except as provided by USA copyright law.

Scripture quotation is taken from the New King James Version except where otherwise noted.

Published in the United States of America
ISBN: 978-0-9892671-8-2 book

ISBN: 978-0-9892671-7-5 ebook Christian Living

Contents:

Foreword			...05
Reviews			...09
Introduction			...13
Chapter	1	Runway of Life	...15
Chapter	2	Exposed!	...25
Chapter	3	Take it off	...30
Chapter	4	Who are You wearing?	...44
Chapter	5	Designers Original	...57
Chapter	6	Confronting the Cover Up	...79
Chapter	7	Being Chosen by God	...83
Chapter	8	Who am I?	...92
Chapter	9	Slips and Falls	...102
Chapter	10	Is Christ Enough?	...112
Chapter	11	YOU Are Enough	...122
Chapter	12	Power Dressing	...134

Foreword

Congratulations, by choosing this book, you have already begun the first step in an amazing life transformation. I truly believe you will not be the same after you have experienced the anointed words of this gifted woman. Those blessed in experiencing the teachings of Karin Griffin understand this book was destined before she even typed her first words. Karin has a deep passion for spiritually empowering women to walk on their rightful path to a victorious life, and she has blessed us with putting her passion in the written word.

Karin bares her soul in this powerful book sharing with her readers how her undeniable faith and love of God has given her the courage to break the bondage of insecurities, self doubt and feelings of inadequacies that were obstructing her vision of God's plans for her life. Through her love of God, she has gained the strength to destroy the barriers of oppression and find the courage to walk in her God given purpose on her life. Her wisdom and testimony will be a blessing to all her readers.

Karin's comparison of our walk in life as our strut on a model's, "Runaway" is powerful and a relevant message in today's society. The reader will gain an in depth, spiritual understanding of how our insecurities can be masked by glitz and glamour which can result in us portraying a false sense of self confidence hiding or worse damaging our true identity.

In this book, Karin walks with the reader page by page as she helps us deepen our relationship with God and find the strength through scripture to remove the glitz and glamour. She directs us on the path to start our new walk to our true self identity. With powerful scripture and words of wisdom, she empowers the reader with the tools to overcome the negative forces that can paralyze us from walking on the path in the vision that God has for our lives.

I have had the opportunity to be under the teachings of Karin in her Women's Mentor Program and at her Heart of a Women's Conference. Her spiritual teachings has encouraged me to grow in my self identity and rediscover my abandoned dreams ultimately creating a new desire in me to walk in victory. My life has been positively changed as a result of encountering this phenomenal woman. I am so excited for her opportunity to share her powerful message in a larger forum.

Each page of this powerful book engages the reader in a spiritual discourse with Karin on a personal level. Karin becomes your personal mentor, from the moment you start reading the book because she shares how she overcomes her insecurities and guides you, through her teachings, to the path to finding God's vision for your life. After reading **NAKED, bare your soul**, you will grow in your true, self identity and recognize it is never to late to re-write your story.

Karin's spiritual voice transcends all boundaries, therefore, no matter where you are in life, this book will empower you beyond imagination, impact your life in a positive way and provide tools for you to overcome obstacles that will clear the path on your **runway** so you can walk in your destiny.

We are so blessed for Karin's voice to emerge with a powerful purpose to transform the lives of women everywhere so we may walk in our God given purpose. She reaches out to women as she walks down the, "**Runway** of life," encouraging and empowering us to take the necessary steps to live our purpose without fear and self doubt.

By picking up this book, you are realizing now is your time to rediscover your dreams, dreams you may have forgotten or gave up on. It is your time to rekindle the desire to find your vision. Under the teachings of this phenomenal author, your life will change in amazing ways. This book will become your handbook on your spiritual walk down the, "**Runway** of life."

God Bless you Karin and thank you for your courage to bare your soul and share your voice with the world.

Angela Gill

REVIEWS

Naked,
bare your soul

By Karin Griffin

"I LOVE this tender, brave, brilliantly yielded woman, a beautiful model of Jesus' gentleness. Karin's transparency about her own insecurities & doubts & feelings of "never being enough" and how all of that conspired to keep her off of her life's Runway will inspire you to throw back the covers & fling open the curtains to your soul so The Light of Jesus's beautiful face can shine into you. The Words from His mouth will give you the strength to put on the new woman and shine as you walk your walk and finish your race with joy!"

Pastor Cindi Townsley
Pastor of 'Believers Center Albuquerque'

REVIEWS

Naked,
bare your soul
By Karin Griffin

"Karin Griffin's book on Naked, bare your soul, is an outstanding book for those who struggle with being the person you were created to be. Karin clearly articulates that in this journey of life, we all will face obstacles and adverse situations but it's not what happens to us that's most important, it's how we respond. This book will equip you with internal strength on how to overcome circumstances that attempt to shut you down. As she bares her soul, after reading this book your faith will soar."

Bishop Sheridan McDaniel
Pastor of 'A Place For Worship'

REVIEWS

Naked,
bare your soul
By Karin Griffin

"Through a process of bare introspection, Karin reconciles and restores readers to the heart of God. As we grapple with our personal inadequacies and internal wrestling, she compels each of us to walk this runway of life with confidence, assurance, and in His pleasure."

Myesha Chaney
Preachers of LA, Recording Artist, Author, Speaker

REVIEWS

Naked,
bare your soul
By Karin Griffin

I love how Karin Griffin is real, raw, and relatable in her book, Naked. Not only does she share how the enemy wants to knock us off our runway called, "life", but she shows us how to embrace who Christ made us to be...unashamedly and confidently. She encourages us to tune out the enemy's voice and tune into God's voice. Karin unviels God's words to gracefully; allowing us to see how it brings life, hope and chance after chance. This book is engaging, powerful, and life changing. I encourage you to read it and allow God to speak to you. And then, as Karin says, put on your stilettos, hold your head up high and go make a difference in this world!

April Osteen Simons
Co Pastor of We are the Church Triumphant, Author

Introduction

My insecurities did not start in my 30's or 40's. It began when I was about 5 years old. As far back as I can remember, I see myself as that little girl who was supposed to be seen but not heard. It wasn't that my parents said that to me, but at some point I put that persona on and allowed it to stay on for many years.

My high school years were very difficult for me. I never seemed to feel comfortable in my own skin. And that traveled with me on through my 20's, 30's and even early 40's. Until I began this journey on the **RUNWAY** that I call life of allowing the real Karin to stand up and raise her voice.

It has not been an easy journey, because sometimes the most difficult thing is exposing you to you. But the beautiful thing I found in this journey of becoming **"NAKED"** and confronting the cover up is that you don't have to do it alone. The Lord has so beautifully graced us with the gift of the Holy Spirit. Who will guide you and lead you down the **Runway** of Life to be free from every stigma, insecurities, inferiority, masks, unworthiness, feelings of abandonment and every other name and title that is contrary to who God so divinely designed you to be.

This book is birthed out of my journey on the **RUNWAY** that I call life. Believing that as I share the revelation, wisdom and guidance given to me by the Holy Spirit you too will be able to stand up in your spiritual stilettos walking freely, securely and assuredly on the foundation of God's word.

My prayer as you read this book is you would grant the precious Holy Spirit to search every area of your life. You will become **"NAKED"** and bare your soul before Him and allow Him to EXPOSE every and anything the enemy has used to hold you captive from walking in the fullness of what you were created to be; on this **RUNWAY** called life.

Will the real you please stand up!
Karin Griffin

Runway of Life

My husband once told me, "The richest place on earth is the graveyard." So many skilled, anointed and gifted people have died, taking with them great aspirations, visions, plans and destiny assignments. Never having the courage, strength, faith or heart, to give birth to the dreams that were at one time burning ever so deep on the inside of them. While living, they watched others from afar and up close, follow through with their dreams. Unfortunately they stood by watching others fulfill the assignment for their lives, while their own dreams lay dormant because of unresolved issues.

You may be asking yourself or thinking, "Karin, what is an issue?" An issue comes in all shapes, forms and sizes and from physical, spiritual and mental aspects. Let's take a look at a few to give you a better idea of what an issue may be: abandonment, un-forgiveness, anger, cutting, irrational expectation of others, hopelessness, trust, divorce, molestation, poverty/lack etc.. My prayer is, as you continue to journey through this book, you will come to the realization; we don't have to allow any issue to hold us down! The word of God informs us in 1 Peter 5:7: *"Casting all your care upon him; for he careth <u>for you.</u>"*

Truly, when we cast our cares upon Him, God is faithful and just to bring healing to those issues. Scripture says, *"Surely He hath borne our griefs, and carried our sorrows [grief, pain, affliction]: yet we did esteem him stricken, smitten of God, and afflicted. But He was wounded for our transgressions, He was bruised for our iniquities: the chastisement of our peace was upon Him; and with His stripes we are healed."* Isaiah 53:4,5.

I am reminded of a woman in scripture that had issues. It's funny because this woman is not known by her name but she is known as the woman with the issue of blood. I am very convinced the Holy Spirit did not inspire this woman to be put in scripture just to give us a good Bible story. He put this woman in scripture so we can draw from her and see that Christ is the healer and is well able to make us whole.

Romans 15:4 Amplified Bible (AMP), *tells us; "For whatever was thus written in former days was written for our instruction, that by [our steadfast and patient] endurance and the encouragement [drawn] from the Scriptures we might hold fast to and cherish hope."*

Join me as we take a look at this woman. I have no doubt after reading her story you will be encouraged like I was and have faith like hers, that you too can be delivered from your issues.

> Luke 8:43-48 King James Version (KJV)
> *"43 And a woman having an issue of blood twelve years, which had spent all her living upon physicians, neither could be healed of any,*
> *44 Came behind him, and touched the border of his garment: and immediately her issue of blood stanched.*
> *45 And Jesus said, Who touched me? When all denied, Peter and they that were with him said, Master, the multitude throng thee and press thee, and sayest thou, Who touched me?*
> *46 And Jesus said, Somebody hath touched me: for I perceive that virtue is gone out of me.*
> *47 And when the woman saw that she was not*

hid, she came trembling, and falling down before him, she declared unto him before all the people for what cause she had touched him, and how she was healed immediately.
48 And he said unto her, Daughter, be of good comfort: thy faith hath made thee whole; go in peace."

As you can see from this story, scripture reveals this woman had an issue, and how she had spent all her money. There was not a doctor that could heal her, deliver her or set her free from her issue, until she came into the presence of the living Savior. Scripture shows us very clearly in verse 45, that there was a multitude of people pressing, pulling and trying to get Jesus' attention. But there was something different about this woman.

I believe she was too desperate to be denied of her healing. From a prophetic standpoint, I believe her desperation is what pulled on Jesus' anointing. I love how in verse 47, after Jesus stopped and asked, 'Who touched me?' She immediately fell at his feet trembling, realizing she had been exposed and could not hide anymore.

Today as this book is in your hand, I believe that some part of you is crying out refusing to be denied of the promises God has ordained for you. Like the lady with the issue, you recognize you can no longer hide and you are ready to encounter Jesus, with the willingness to fall at His feet and allow Him to heal your very issue.

The beauty we see in the life of this woman is really sealed in verse 48. Not only did Jesus heal her issue, but Jesus also touched her and made her whole.

You see my friends according to scripture, Christ died for our, "Total Deliverance and healing from Every Issue." Unfortunately we've been taught for so long….knowingly and unknowingly, it's not cool to EXPOSE your inner scars, pains and vulnerabilities. So, through the process of time, ups and downs, we learn to pull our big girl panties up and keep on moving. Never confronting the ULTIMATE cover up. We learn to mask ourselves for so long, day in and day out, until one day we wake up and we no longer can identify with the person in the mirror.

We can see that example very clear in James 1:24. It says to us; *"...and, after looking at himself, goes away and immediately forgets what he looks like."* (NIV).

Unfortunately, this happens to so many as they walk this **Runway** of life. So often, because we lose sense of who we are, dreams that were once ever so vivid and clear, are now nowhere to be found. Not even in a distant memory. Somehow, we lost focus. Instead of dealing with the problems and underlying issues that caused the dreams to fade away, we continue the cycle of cover up and mask ourselves one more day, as we step onto this **Runway** called life.

> Jeremiah 29:11 (NIV) says, *"For I know the plans I have for you, declares the Lord, plans to prosper you and not to harm you, plans to give you hope and a future."*

Gods plans for us are far greater than we can ever dream or imagine. We would be totally blown away if we could really see in the natural our potential and the wonderful plan God has divinely designed for our lives. I remember so vividly one Sunday as my husband was giving his talk. He said, "If we truly were living up to our potential, we would be unrecognizable!"

My prayer for you and every reader is that your days of covering up will come to a screeching halt, allowing you to see your potential and become unrecognizable! It's time to confront the ultimate cover up. Allowing the Holy Spirit to EXPOSE YOU. Allowing yourself to be, (laid open for viewing, unconcealed and vulnerable) before the Lord. Freeing yourself from every trap the enemy has set for your life.

Remember, Jesus is the Author of our, "Life's Story," and His plan for us is to prosper and give us a victorious ending. We must see our life's story as a # 1 N.Y. Times Best Seller.

The enemy's job is to keep us blinded to the fact that our God is all knowing. You see we don't have to duck and dive from the very God that uniquely created us. Creation itself cannot hide from God. Scripture tells us in Job 26:6, *"Hell is naked before him, and destruction hath no covering."*

So get this, according to our God, even Hell itself is **Naked** before Him…let's just park right there for a moment and rest on that thought. The Word of God goes on to say even destruction is laid uncovered. So my friend, who are we to try to hide from a Great Big, All Knowing, All Powerful God. IT'S TIME TO STRIP DOWN, UNCOVER AND JUST GET **NAKED** BEFORE HIM.

It's time to get busy and begin taking off the layers that have held you captive for way too long. When we die we have to die empty. We should have totally acted out and filled to the full, every plan and purpose God has ordained for our lives. Our mindset must be, not one treasure our Beautiful Savior has entrusted to us, will die with us. It's time to get **exposed!** Lights, camera action!

Will the real you please stand up!

What issue stagnates my runway walk?

Exposed!

Hebrews 4:13 says, *"Nothing in all creation is hidden from God's sight. Everything is uncovered and laid bare before the eyes of him to whom we must give account."* (NIV).

What is even more mind blowing is one day we will all have to give an account for what we did with the gift and talents God ordained for us to flourish in. So why not unveil and confront the cover up, because as we see; nothing in creation is hidden. All is uncovered and laid open before Him, so its time out for hiding, we may as well get **EXPOSED**.

Jeremiah 23:23,24; tells us; *"Am I a God who is near, declares the LORD, "And not a God far off? Can anyone hide in hiding places So I do not see him? Declares the LORD. Do I not fill the heavens and the earth? Declares the LORD."* (NASB).

Jeremiah 16:17, says; *"For My gaze takes in all their ways. They are not concealed from*

Me, and their guilt is not hidden from My sight." (HCSB).

I love how 1 Peter 5:8, (NIV) reminds us how we must be alert and aware of the enemy in our lives. *"Be alert and of sober mind. Your enemy the devil prowls around like a roaring lion looking for someone to devour."*

John 10:10, (NIV) shows us, *"The thief comes only to steal and kill and destroy; I have come that they may have life, and have it to the full."* So, no matter what the attack we WIN! Gods Perfect Plan for you is to have a Full and Fruitful life. He had a plan for you before you were ever born. Your life story was written before you were without form, and get this; Your Life Story is a # 1 N.Y. Times Best Seller.

Psalm 139:16, (NIV) says; *"Your eyes saw my unformed body; all the days ordained for me were written in your book before one of them came to be."*

Everything about you was written in a book before you were ever born and you know what that means; you have the **leading role!** So lets get the camera rolling, we don't have time to waste.

We must remember that absolutely nothing about us is hidden from God, or catches him off guard. So do not allow the lies and accusations of the enemy to keep you in hiding because the Lord knows right where you are.

Come take a look with me as
we unveil more scripture..........

Will the real you please stand up!

Expose *your plan for me Lord*

Take it Off

On my **Runway** I had to realize very quickly that I could not believe the lies of the enemy. One of the things I had to work on, was not allowing the enemy's lies to seduce me out of my place and position, causing me to put on things to cover up my **Naked**ness and Vulnerability. Scripture gives us a great example of how this can occur through the life of Adam and Eve. Take a look with me at, "THE ULTIMATE FIG LEAF COVER UP."

> Look closely with me at Genesis 3 from the NIV version:
> *1 Now the serpent was more crafty than any of the wild animals the Lord God had made. He said to the woman, "Did God really say, 'You must not eat from any tree in the garden'?"*
> *2 The woman said to the serpent, "We may eat fruit from the trees in the garden,*
> *3 but God did say, 'You must not eat fruit from the tree that is in the middle of the garden, and you must not touch it, or you will die.'"*
> *4 "You will not certainly die," the serpent said to the woman.*

5 "For God knows that when you eat from it your eyes will be opened, and you will be like God, knowing good and evil."
6 When the woman saw that the fruit of the tree was good for food and pleasing to the eye, and also desirable for gaining wisdom, she took some and ate it. She also gave some to her husband, who was with her, and he ate it.
7 Then the eyes of both of them were opened, and they realized they were naked; so they sewed fig leaves together and made coverings for themselves.

Just take a moment and say to yourself, "Now that was the ultimate cover up." Not only was it the ultimate cover up, it was the first **runway** cover up from a spiritual standpoint. They took fig leaves to cover up their **naked**ness. They thought they were covering their mess, weaknesses, insecurities, and everything else they felt or knew was contrary to the will of God for their lives. They did not want to be exposed to themselves, others, but moreover, to God.

Scripture tells us we don't need to hide from God because He already knows everything about us. Once again as I shared before, *"Nothing in all creation is hidden from God's sight. Everything is uncovered and laid bare before the eyes of Him to whom we must give account"* (Hebrews 4:13, NIV).

Let's look a little bit further at the ultimate cover up:

Genesis 3:8-10; (NIV) *"Then the man and his wife heard the sound of the Lord God as he was walking in the garden in the cool of the day, and they hid from the Lord God among the trees of the garden. But the Lord God called to the man, 'Where are you?' He answered, 'I heard you in the garden, and I was afraid because I was naked; so I hid.' "*

We see how Satan came into Adam and Eve's life to destroy the call God had placed upon them. They were fearful when they realized their **naked**ness and therefore, put on fig leaves to cover their **naked**ness. Sadly enough, this is a picture of what happens to us. Instead of allowing our self to come clean and admit our being **naked** before our all knowing all loving God, we, just like Adam and Eve, fall short or lose sight of our Spiritual **Runway** and try to cover up our...

Nakedness   Insecurities
Shortcoming   Hurts
Mistakes   Struggles
Faults   Lack of faith
Weaknesses   ETC....

But what I love so much about this picture, is God came looking for them. And, just like He came looking for them, He is looking for us. Calling out for us to draw close to Him, so He can direct us out of every situation, every slip, fall and spiritual blooper, while on this **Runway** called life. He knows we won't get it right all the time. He knows everything about us, as He did Adam and Eve, yet, He came looking for them. Even as you are reading this, I believe you are sensing His promptings, and His beckoning for you to come out, come out from wherever you are.

We also see God asking Adam and Eve where are you? Not that God did not know where they were. God knew exactly where they were. It was more about Him finding out if they knew where they were and, if they were even aware of how they allowed themselves to get into that place of hiding and cover up.

So, yes again, I don't believe God was asking Adam and Eve where they were because He needed to know. He was asking Adam and Eve, "Where are you?" Because he wanted them to know where they were. I believe He put that question to them, and He is also asking you:
- *Do you know where you are?*
- *Do you know the situation you're in?*
- *Are you aware the enemy has come in to cause you to go run and hide?*
- *Do you know you are off the Runway of life I designed for you?*
- *Do you know you have put on a cover up, something I didn't give you?*

God loved them so much; He wanted them to become uniquely aware of their current situation. That's just how much our God loves us. He will come and find us, challenging us to confront and locate our current state or situation. My question to you, before we go any further is:
- *Where are you?*
- *What is your current situation?*
- *Where are you on your Runway called life?*

As you walk this **Runway** called life, be reminded that nothing, absolutely nothing can separate us, can separate you, from the love of God. Scripture says it best.....

> Romans 8:38,39, (NIV) explains; *"For I am convinced that neither death nor life, neither angels nor demons, neither the present nor the future, nor any powers, neither height nor depth, nor anything else in all creation, will be able to separate us from the love of God that is in Christ Jesus our Lord."*

There's no need to hide. As you are turning the pages of this book, if you are hiding behind a cover up, come out of your hiding place. Take off those fig leaves because He loves you unconditionally!

> Romans 5:8, (NIV) tells us; *"But God demonstrates his own love for us in this: While we were still sinners, Christ died for us."*

Even when we mess up, God still loves us. He's going to come looking for you, just bare yourself before Him. Confront your cover up! He did not come to condemn, He came to heal, set free and deliver.

Romans 8:1: (NIV), *"Therefore, there is now no condemnation for those who are in Christ Jesus,"*

Ephesians 3:19, (NIV) says; *"and to know this love that surpasses knowledge - that you may be filled to the measure of all the fullness of God."*

Jesus came to save and seek those that were lost, and that's what we see in the Garden of Eden. Jesus went looking for Adam and He went looking for Eve WITH UNCONDITIONAL LOVE. Let's look a little closer at the scripture in Genesis.

Genesis 3:10-11, (NIV) tells us; *"He answered, "I heard you in the garden, and I was afraid because I was naked; so I hid." And he said, "Who told you that you were naked? Have you eaten from the tree that I commanded you not to eat from?""*

We see here Adam saying he heard the Voice of God. He heard the Voice of God right where he was in the garden; but, he was afraid. Let's park right there. From the moment we don't confront our cover up, while walking this **Runway** of life, we give the spirit of fear permission to seduce us out of our rightful place with God and; our rightful place on our **Runway**.

Gods Word says that He never gave us fear, and, He calls fear out and identifies it as a spirit.

> 2 Timothy 1:7, (HCSB); *"For God has not given us a spirit of fearfulness, but one of power, love, and sound judgment."*

When God gave Adam dominion over the Garden of Eden, to rule, reign, multiply and have authority, replenish and subdue the earth. The garden belonged to Adam and Eve to control, but, when they allowed the cover up to take place, they allowed the enemy to put doubt, unbelief and fear in them. Doubt, unbelief and fear caused them to cover up their **naked**ness and they ran and hid from God. The enemy's job is to constantly come against us so we would coward down and draw back from fulfilling our God-given purpose, and our God-given destiny. So, my question to you now is, **"What are you wearing?"** Have you confronted your cover up? Where are you? The enemy knows God created you for greatness!

Genesis chapter 1 verse 27 & 28, (NIV) says, *"So God created mankind in his own image, in the image of God he created them; male and female he created them. God blessed them and said to them, 'Be fruitful and increase in number; fill the earth and subdue it. Rule over the fish in the sea and the birds in the sky and over every living creature that moves on the ground.'"*

After God created you and I in His image, He blessed us. Now let's park right there for a moment and just meditate on the fact God created us just like him and then pronounced a blessing upon us. Wow...wow. WOW! He blessed us:
- *To be fruitful*
- *To fill the earth*
- *To have dominion*
- *To rule*

Scripture tells us the heaven and the earth is the Lord's but He has given the earth to us to rule.

Deuteronomy 10:14 says, *"To the LORD your God belong the heavens, even the highest heavens, the earth and everything in it."* (NIV).

Psalms 115:16 tells us; *"The highest heavens belong to the LORD, but the earth he has given to mankind."* (NIV).

The enemy is after your destiny. The enemy's job is to cause us to run and hide, so we will put things on that does not belong to us. This causes us to cover up, hide, and be afraid to walk in our God-given authority, which will allow us to fulfill our destiny. Take a moment and say to yourself, "No more hiding for me because I've been made in the image of the Almighty God."

The thing that gets me the most is that Adam made it very clear he was hiding and, he was **naked**. Adam proved this when he said to God; not only did we hide because we were afraid, but we hid because we were **NAKED!** As if God didn't already know, because, "God knows all and sees all."

And I love it!!! God said, who told you that? Well blow me down, that just blows my mind. God looks in the face of Adam and challenges him with the question, **"Who told you that you are naked?"** You see God sees us in our finished state. He does not see us as we see ourselves, but he sees us, as we will be.

So often we believe the lies of the enemy or our current situation, and like Adam, we begin to cover up. Adam, used fig leaves, but as the late Joan Rivers coined it... Who are you wearing?

"What are you wearing to cover up?" Are you wearing hurt, pain, disappointment, resentment, lack, weariness, sickness, brokenness and loss of security?

Whatever it is, it is not too big for our God to handle. You see the enemy's job is to shut us down, cause us to hide, make us feel embarrassed. He does his best to convince us we are unworthy, unloved, and, persuades us to feel inadequate. But I decree, and I declare, as you turn the pages of this book, you will recognize that Worthy is The Lamb. And because of the Blood of Jesus; we have the unique and glorious ability to confront every cover up. So every stronghold, barrier and mountain would be made low, and, we can walk victoriously as a victor.

We can walk fulfilling the God given assignment and the mandate that has been placed upon our lives. Take a moment to write down the areas in your life where you have felt unworthy like you've had to cover up, and together let's confront it.

I will confront:

_____

_____

As we walk this **Runway** called life as if wearing our spiritual stilettos, we can never forget we have been CHOSEN!

Scripture tells us in John 15:16: *"You didn't choose me. I chose you. I appointed you to go and produce lasting fruit, so that the Father will give you whatever you ask for, using my name."* (NLT).

The thought provoking question for you and I as we come to the place of confronting our cover up, along with the reality check that the enemy will do all he can to cause us to run into hiding as he did with Adam and Eve. Isn't it true we, you and I, were CHOSEN to walk in dominion and kingdom Authority?

Will the real you please stand up?

What will I take off?

Who are you Wearing?

"Who are you wearing?" Seems to be a common question on the **runway**s these days. We see actors, musicians and celebrities walking the Red Carpet during award season year in and year out it never fails. Whether it's the Oscars, Grammys, MTV awards, BET awards, Emmy awards, Gospel Music Awards, VMA's or the Country Music awards they all have one thing in common. During the pre-show where every celebrity walks the Red Carpet they will be asked the question. "What are you wearing?" Or, "Who are you wearing?" Well my dear friends, my thought provoking question to you, as you flip the pages of this book is, **"Who are you wearing?"**

The **runway**s are filled with men and women that have hired stylists to dress them so they can look beautiful on the outside, neglecting to focus on the inside and deal with the very issues that are weighing them down. We can go from one tabloid to another and see men and women who make millions and millions of dollars, having sufficient money to eat at the best restaurants. Sleep in the most exclusive hotels, travel the world, dress in high end vintage clothing and wear designer shoes. They are able to hire the best and most well-known make-up artists and hairstylists. They walk the Red Carpet with their heads lifted high waiting for the next reporter to ask, "Who are you wearing?" While on the inside many of them are hurting, broken, discouraged, troubled, saddened, lonely, broke, busted, disgusted and in despair. As life continues to hit them with its best shot on every turn.

That person may even be you! You might be the very person that is confident on the outside; having the ability to win an Oscar Award because of the performance you put on day in and day out. You may even be able to win a Grammy because you are singing a good song. But truly that song is really a facade because you refuse to confront the cover up and deal with the inner dealings that cripples you. The debilitating pain in your heart and mind that holds you captive from fulfilling your God given destiny, stagnating you from walking in the fullness of what your God has created you to do.

I just choose to believe that nothing happens by accident. You see, everything was pre ordained before the foundation of time by our True and Living God. God knew that at this very moment, this very hour, this very day, this very second; you would be holding this particular book in your hand to provoke you with this very question; "Who am I wearing?"

Scripture makes it very clear in Proverbs 16:9, (NLT); *"We can make our plans, but the Lord determines our steps."* So often we go through life putting on things God did not ordain for us.

The Bible says in Proverbs 23:7a (AKJV); *"For as he thinks in his heart, so is he."* Not your heart that pumps blood but your mind, your soul, your intellect. What are you thinking, because what you think, you will become.

Have you ever noticed those same beautiful and amazing models and actors that walk the **runway** or red carpet, are often, "EXPOSED" by the very people that applaud and build them up today? Those same people will turn around and bring them down in the next tabloid article on the newsstand, iPhone, iPad or a gossip show tomorrow. Photographing them without their make-up, expensive jewels, designer clothing, nor designer shoes.

Those tabloid gives us the opportunity to get a birds eye view of them totally unmasked, unveiled not looking anything like what we see when they are at their best. They are caught off guard and totally exposed to ridicule, as total strangers take the opportunity to sensationalize them. Not only do the strangers focus on lurid news and gossip in order to bring shame and humiliation to them at the expense of making money or better ratings, but they have no regard to how this will affect their emotional wellbeing. More often than not, this negative exposure and press will cause a person to continue the cycle of daily covering up to avoid the pain, ridicule, scrutiny and negative press from the accuser or the exposer. Thus, continuing a charade that only keeps them in a place of bondage.

Like theses performers, do you get up and go to work every day with your facade on, but at night you come home and you feel like the enemy is taking over every aspect and every part of your life? I'm reminded of the scripture from Psalms 40:11,12, when David cried out to God…*"Now God, don't hold out on me, don't hold back your passion. Your love and truth are all that keeps me together. When troubles ganged up* on me, a mob of sins past counting, I was so swamped by guilt I couldn't see my way clear. More guilt was in my heart than hair on my head, so heavy the guilt that my heart gave out."

Right now, as you're turning the pages of this book, while you are unmasked, trying to confront the cover ups no longer on the red carpet. No longer putting on your Oscar performances. No longer singing your beautiful song-and you may feel like trouble has ganged up on you or you may feel like your troubles are more than the hairs upon your head. I know, your'e saying to yourself, "Boy that's a whole lot of trouble I have to face!"

I'm here to encourage you! Trouble won't last always. Walk with me to Luke 12:7, (NIV) the Bible tells us, *"Indeed, the very hairs of your head are all numbered. Don't be afraid; you are worth more than many sparrows."*

For many years I was that person. Getting up daily, putting on a smile, while I was slowly dying on the inside. I had somehow loss every sense of who I was. As I daily found myself in a place of battling insecurity, feelings of rejection, abandonment, and low self-esteem. I carried with me a sense of inadequacy. Never feeling good enough, smart enough, pretty enough, worthy enough, to birth out the dreams I had hidden in my heart.

I had somehow lost all sense of who I was from a very young age. Yet at the same time I was looking for the confidence I needed, while trying to have the courage to break free of all that had me bound. Knowing daily I was covering up; I wanted so badly to break free. I just did not know how to confront the cover up. I had lived in that place of masking my pain and insecurities for so long, I had no idea how to find my way out.

The thought of unveiling or exposing my inner scars was far beyond my reach, until I became acquainted with the Word of God. As I began my journey of confronting the cover up I did not know many scriptures. But the few I had, began to change my view on who I was, through the eyes of Christ. As I searched the scriptures, I began to discover my worth and my value through the eyes of Christ.

One day I came across Psalm 139:13,14 (KJV); *"For thou hast possessed my reins: thou hast covered me in my mother's womb. I will praise thee; for I am fearfully and wonderfully made: marvelous are thy works; and that my soul knoweth right well."*

Through that scripture I was challenged and I had to get my mind around the fact; God gave thought when he created me and everything God did was excellent. So, that meant; "I" had to be excellent. At that moment I began the journey of getting the thoughts about myself to line up with the Word of God. The Bible says what I think is what I will become. Because my self-talk to myself had become so negative, without even realizing it, I began to agree with the outside voices of society. Without even realizing it, I had rewritten the script God had ordained for my life. And, my script looked nothing like what God's Word says about me. It is said that 70 percent of our self-talk, the conversations we have in our head with our selves is negative. So daily, 70 percent of what I said and how I saw myself was contrary to that which God said I was.

The Word of God tells us what is in our HEART (mind, thoughts, intellect) we will speak. And, I had become a fool to believe my own negative self-talk. I did not even realize I was in bondage. I was trapped and ensnared by my own thoughts and words. I was carrying, or should I say, I was walking, my **RUNWAY**, sporting baggage that did not belong to me.

> Proverbs 6:2 (NIV), *states; "You have been trapped by what you said; ensnared by the words of your mouth."*

> KJV of Proverbs 28:26 says, *"He that trusteth in his own heart is a fool: but whoso walketh wisely, he shall be delivered."*

Before I even knew it, I had become captive, under control of my own thoughts. I was in bondage to my own words and thoughts. You may ask, what is Bondage? Bondage is the state of being under control of a force or influence. Bondage is also the state of one who is bound as in captivity or slavery. So in order for me to be free, I had to begin to renew my thoughts and my daily conversations about myself; to myself and, be reminded of who I am through the eyes of Christ.

> Remember Psalm 139:13,14 (KJV) says; *"For thou hast possessed my reins: thou hast covered me*

in my mother's womb. I will praise thee; for I am fearfully and wonderfully made: marvelous are thy works; and that my soul knoweth right well."

Daily I began to speak the Word of God over myself. Matthew 12:37 (NIV), tells us; *"For by your words you will be acquitted, and by your words you will be condemned."*

My thoughts, which became my self-talk, had me condemned for so many years; but daily I began to fill my mouth with what the Lord says about me. Going back to the 'Original Manuscript,' written in my life story daily. I realized when my self-talk wanted to speak condemnation; something would rise up on the inside of me and say, NO, NO, NO GIRL, YOU HAVE BEEN ACQUITTED! The self-talk slowly began to flip and now, my self-talk is about 70/30. 70 percent positive confessions. I have to be honest; I'm still working on the 30 percent. I'm still a work in progress!

The Scriptures slowly but surely began to transform me from the inside out. God had His hand on me and He covered and protected me from my mother's womb. I know that may seem elementary to some that are reading this, but just park on that thought for a moment.

We serve a God that cares that much about us. From the womb he had us on His mind! Wow, Wow, Wow. Once you get that revelation, Psalm 139:14 really comes alive. Because when you know God had your back from the womb, you can't help but praise Him and get the full awareness and picture that no matter what society, friends, mother or father say or think about you, you were and are truly FEARFULLY AND WONDERFULLY MADE. When you get that in your heart, you will get up every day on your **Runway** called life, look at yourself in the mirror and say, "MARVELOUS, GIRL YOU ARE JUST MARVELOUS. YOU ARE GODS WORK." I am simply MARVELOUS and my soul knows it right well.

Will the real you please stand up!

Who am I wearing?

What should I be wearing?

Before getting a hold of the Word of God, my outlook on life was so bad. My posture was humped over. I don't know about you, but on a **runway**, I have never seen a model wear a designer's original humped over. Those women and men are strutting the **runway**s with their heads held so high, no one can tell them anything. They know they are 'Hot!' They are confident they look good. Walking bent over does not even enter their mind. Well, to the contrary on my **RUNWAY** called life. I had put on the baggage of the world for so long, my posture was bent over from a spiritual aspect. Looking up had not even crossed my mind. But, when I got ahold of the Word, daily the Word of God began to pick me up from a bent over state of shame, hopelessness and despair.

The Word began to speak to the very core of my being and say; "Karin; **thou art loosed!** It's time for you to get up on that **RUNWAY** called life and strut your stuff." God, by His spirit began to speak to me in the very still but All-knowing voice. "Girl, don't you know you are a designers original and I have created you for greatness?" As days and months went by, I came to a place where I began to learn how not to underestimate the Hand of God on my life.

Job 12:10, (NIV) says, *"In His hand is the life of every creature and the breath of all mankind."*

Throughout scripture the Bible speaks of, "The right hand of God." The right hand in Biblical symbolism means strength, honor, and power. The hand of God in scripture always saves, protects, provides, delivers, or fights for us.

Exodus 15:6 tells us; *"Your right hand, O Lord, has become glorious in power: Your right hand, O Lord, has dashed the enemy in pieces."* (KJ2000B).

Psalms 16:8 says; *"I have set the Lord always before me: Because he is at my right hand, I shall not be moved."* (AKJV).

Psalms 20:6 says; *"Now I know that the Lord saves his anointed; He will answer him from his holy heaven with the saving strength of His right hand."* (KJ2000B).
Psalms 60:5 reads; *"That Your beloved may be*

delivered; save with your right hand, and hear me." (KJ2000B).

Psalms 16:11 says; *"You will show me the path of life; In your presence is fullness of joy; at your right hand there are pleasures forevermore."* (KJ2000B).

I began to find strength and courage knowing the Hand of God and not man's hand was on my life. I soon learned I served a God that thought so much about me according to scripture. He even engraved my name, yes my name, in His Hand. It's funny because we are in a season in life where tattoos are a big thing now. We see men and women who are in love getting each other's name tattooed on them. But guess what my God, the creator of the universe, thinks so much about me. He engraved my name in His Hand; symbolizing how much He loves me and everything about me was before Him.

Meaning, nothing about me is hidden from Him. He carries my name as an engraved picture in His hand. Wow, let's just park right there for a moment. Doesn't that just blow your mind? He loves us so much, He took time and engraved our name in the palm of His

Hand. The thought alone of my name being engraved in His Hand, gave me the fuel and ammunition to daily get up, hit my **RUNWAY** of life, and allow myself to become more vulnerable and **NAKED**. That thought also gives me the ability to free myself from all that had me bound and stay true to the original manuscript written of me.

> Isaiah 49:16 (NIV), says: *"See, I have engraved you on the palms of my hands; your walls are ever before me."*

I knew that in order to stay vulnerable and **NAKED** before the Lord, I had to allow the Word of God to totally transform me. I found in scripture a story of a woman that had been bent over for 18 long years. It's in Luke 13:11; *"And behold, there was a woman who had had a disabling spirit for eighteen years. She was bent over and could not fully straighten herself."* (ESV).

1. This woman's disability or crippled state from a prophetic stand point, deals with the fact she may have needed physical, mental and social healing.
2. Her twisted body permanently bent towards the ground from a prophetic stand point shows she may

have come to a place where she had lost all hope.

3. Her posture was a prophetic picture that she had no strength to pick herself up.

I could so identify with this woman. Just like her, throughout the years, I had allowed myself to become disabled from a spiritual aspect. I had become stagnant and totally paralyzed to all that had me bound. My countenance and posture outwardly was an absolute charade. Because in solitude and behind closed doors, I had lost all hope and had no strength, in the natural, to set myself free. But the beautiful thing is, I did not have to set myself free, because my freedom from all, not some, but all strongholds and bondage was taken care of over 2000 years ago because of the blood of Jesus! And what He did on Calvary for you and for me!

Scripture says in John 8:36, *"So if the Son makes you free, you will be free indeed."* (NASB). Like this woman in scripture, I wanted so badly to be free. I was so intrigued by the story of this woman 18 years of being bound. So I began to look a little closer to see what scripture revealed about this woman's situation and how it could possibly apply to my life.

And, as I began to look a little further in the scriptures about this woman's situation to find out how it could possibly apply to me. I was amazed, come, take a walk with me and see what I found...

> Luke 13:10-12, (ESV) reads; *"Now he was teaching in one of the synagogues on the Sabbath. And behold, there was a woman who had had a disabling spirit for eighteen years. She was bent over and could not fully straighten herself. When Jesus saw her, He called her over and said to her, "Woman, you are freed from your disability."*

Please, just for a moment let me get a little technical with this scripture.

Luke 13:10: Jesus was teaching in the synagogue. In modern terms that would be He was teaching in (The Church). This shows although this woman may have lost hope and faith by her actions and her posture, somewhere deep down inside, she knew God was not through with her yet. And, I can just hear her say; "If I could just get in His presence, possibly, I could be set free." I could so identify with that picture.

Although there were many seasons where I felt all hope was gone. I can remember spending many nights crying myself to sleep. Struggling with my internal private and hidden battles, totally unrecognizable to my own self. Somewhere deep down inside my soul, I knew I had so much more to offer than what I was giving; because of my issues and disabilities that had me bent over spirituality. Like this woman, I knew I needed to be stripped **NAKED** and loosed from the strongholds that had me so bound. I began to do all I could to get in the presence of God. Even when I felt all hope was gone, I continued to pursue His presence.

I came across the scripture of Abraham. The Bible says against all hope; Abraham believed.

> Romans 4:18 says; *"Even when there was no reason for hope, Abraham kept hoping--believing that he would become the father of many nations. For God had said to him, 'That's how many descendants you will have!'"* (NLT).

As I searched the scriptures I saw when there was no reason to hope, Abraham still believed. Now think about it, let's keep it real. The average man would have said, "You have got to be kidding me! My wife at 90 will become pregnant and at 100 years old, I'll be able to get her pregnant? Get out of here." We must never forget God himself wrote the script and what God has for you, no demon in hell can stop it!

We have to have the same faith as Abraham and Sarah, when all hope is gone, hope again. Let me say it one more time. When all hope is gone, hope again. You may be in a hopeless situation right now, bent over feeling like you can never be loosed from the grip of the enemy; the dream will never come alive, your body will never be healed. You'll never get that degree, you'll never buy that house, and you'll never amount to anything. Whatever it may be, I say to you, today; hope again. Hope again girl, hope again.

Like Abraham, this bent over woman's action shows she yet believed she could be set free; **even after 18 years of being bent over.** What we see by her action is:
- *She was seeking the Face of God.*
- *She was in the Church were the Word was being given.*
- *She knew she would meet Jesus there.*
- *She had faith He could heal her.*

Abraham and this woman was working the word:

Hebrews 11:6, (KJV) tells us; *"But without faith it is impossible to please Him: for he that cometh to God must believe that he is, and that he is a rewarder of them that diligently seek him."*

Hebrews 11:1 (KJV) says; *"Now faith is the substance of things hoped for, the evidence of things not seen."*

As I became more acquainted with the Word of God, like this bent over woman, I began to build my faith and have hope beyond hope. No matter what it looked like, I had to keep my eyes on Jesus. Hebrews 12:2 tells us we must look to Jesus; He is the Author and the Finisher, the Perfecter of our faith.

Jeremiah 1:5 tells us; *"Before I formed thee in embryo I knew thee; and before thou was born I sanctified thee, and I ordained thee a prophet to the nations."* (WBT).

When I read Jeremiah 1:5, I realized just like you will realize as you continue to read, we are a Divine Design; created by the Creator of the universe! Think about it. We were not some afterthought God just decided to throw in creation as a last minute thought. NO, NO, NO! Our God, the Master Designer, created us with a plan to do something great and fulfill a work that no one else could do but you or me.

I think of some of the greatest designers of our times. When they create or design a dress, they often times have someone on their mind who they want to wear what they are creating. Its funny as I am writing this, one of the greatest designers of our times just recently passed away. As I watched a segment about him, they said he was a master designer and designed dresses for all of the First Ladies in his era. He will always be remembered as a well-known designer. The reporter said Oscar De La Renta would design a garment or ball gown to suit the person's personality. He created many beautiful gowns for Nancy Reagan, Barbra Bush and Hillary Clinton.

When you think about it, each of these ladies have very different personalities and body forms, but yet, because he was a 'master designer,' he took great care in crafting a garment to suit each person. How much more would not the creator of all creation, take time and design a well thought out plan when creating both you and I. He is the Master Designer. And guess what? He has a Master Plan for you and me. We just need to stay to His script and plan He has designed specifically for us.

Just like Jeremiah, before he was ever born, God had a plan for him and He has a plan for us. So, no matter what your situation is today, dare to have hope beyond hope.

> Jeremiah 29:11 (NIV) tells us, *"For I know the plans I have for you, declares the Lord, plans to Prosper you and not to harm you, plans to give you hope and a future."*

Let's look back at Luke 13:11. The Bible points out the length of time she was bent over, 18 very long years. That is a long time for someone to be in a posture of no hope. What this shows is, it does not matter...
- *How long we have been down.*
- *How deep a hole we find ourselves in.*
- *How dark our sin may be.*
- *God is yet able to meet us there.*

Luke 13:11 also says the woman was so bent over; "SHE" could in no way raise herself up. This shows that weaknesses cannot be dealt with in our own strength. So often, because of shame, pride and our own issues, we try to handle situations in our own strength, ability and power. However, in every weakness we have, there is the Lord's strength to strengthen us.

2 Corinthians 12: 9 & 10 (NKJV) states; *"And He said unto me, "My grace is sufficient for you, for My strength is made perfect in weakness." Therefore most gladly I will rather boast in my infirmities, that the power of Christ may rest upon me. Therefore I take pleasure in infirmities, in reproaches, in needs, in persecutions, in distresses, for Christ sake. For when I am weak, then I am strong."* We must learn to find our strength in Christ Jesus.

Isaiah 41:10 (NIV) says, *"So do not fear, for I am with you; do not be dismayed, for I am your God. I will strengthen you and help you; I will uphold you with my righteous right hand."* Also, I love that Ephesians 6:10 tells us to... Finally, be strengthened by the Lord and by His vast strength!

The beauty of Luke 13:12 shows us that Jesus saw the bent over woman, in her broken, bent and stricken state and, He called for her. Just as Jesus called her, He is calling you and I.

Jesus saw beyond her bent over state. He saw her **NAKED** and bare, beyond the surface, and spoke to the situation and caused her to be loosed from her infirmity. You see Jesus did not have to ask her any questions. He already knew her situation and, He was ready to meet her every need. He was able to bring restoration and deliverance to the very thing that had her bound. When we see Jesus speaking to her dis-ability/crippled state, and command she be loosed. I'm reminded in scripture of when Jesus told the disciples, "Let's cross over to the other side."

They all went into the boat and a great storm arose. Water began covering the boat, to the point they felt they were going to drown. I know the disciples must have been saying, 'Now I know I did not forsake all to follow You and come out here to die, while You are asleep on a pillow at the bottom of this boat. Don't you see what's going on with me?' Just as myself, and even the disciples, you may feel like a storm has hit your life.

Maybe it has been one storm after another and you're like, 'When is this going to end? Jesus must be oblivious of the storms in my life.' But what we will notice is, when the disciples ran to Jesus and woke him, in Matthew He said to them, *"...Why are you afraid, you men of little faith?" Then He got up and rebuked the winds and the sea, and it became perfectly calm. The men were amazed, and said, 'What kind of man is this, that even the winds and the sea obey Him?'"*

Let's park for a moment on that thought. The fact Jesus spoke to the winds and the sea and they obeyed his voice... Whatever wind or storm that is raging in your life, let the Spirit of God's Word speak life and bring restoration to any and every situation that has you bound. I prophetically declare by the authority of Jesus Christ that you are loosed!

I also love how the disciples asked, "What manner of man is this that even winds and the sea obey His voice?" That same manner of Man that is the True and Living God will bring to silence every raging storm in your life that is contrary to the will of God for your life. Just as He spoke to the winds and they were silenced, he spoke to the woman's infirmity and she was made whole. I dare you to open your mouth and speak over every storm and wind and, decree today; 'you will be made whole.'

> Now, let's look at Luke 13:13, *"Then he put his hands on her, and immediately she straightened up and praised God."* (NIV).

Jesus spoke over her in verse 12 and commanded that she be loosed. Then He touched her and the Bible says immediately, instantly, presently she was made straight. Able to look up, dream again and walk through every open door God had ordained for her to walk through, confidently and victoriously, as she walked her **Runway** called life. Because God is not a respecter of persons, I decree and declare that by the time you come to the end of this book, your faith will be enlarged. Your hope in Christ will be renewed; your posture will be restored. And, you will stand up straight and glorify your God as never before.

Like this woman, there was a season when I had been crippled in my situation for so long. I felt if I ever tried to rise up from my bent position to go and seek for the Lord, or get in His presence or, if I dared to expose my scars, shame, weakness and shortcomings; I would only open myself up to ridicule and embarrassment.

But I am alive to share with you my friend, the devil is a liar! In John 8:44 the devil is called, "The father of lies." The enemy will do everything in his power to keep you from confronting the cover up so he can keep you bound until he is ready to expose you. I took the chance and confronted my cover up and allowed the Holy Spirit to give me a spiritual makeover.

So often as we walk this **Runway** called life, we get up, dress up, put our faces on, and go through our day with our charade. But at night, we come home and feel like the walls are closing in on us as we channel surf, looking for anything that will allow an escape. Meanwhile the enemy is taking over and gaining ground in every aspect and every part of our life such as our:

- *Marriage*
- *Singleness*
- *Finances*
- *Peace*
- *Self-worth*
- *Identity*
- *Dreams*
- *Children*
- *Relationships*
- *Health*

Sometimes our disabilities are so deep, just like the woman in Luke 13:11; our posture has been down so long, the possibility of looking up is not even in our future plans. The dirt on the ground has been your constant view, and you are unable to see the smiles on people's faces. You are unable to reach for the sky. Being bent over has blocked every view of dreams and all possibilities God has set before you. But, we serve a God that loves us so much! He paid the price for our emotional healing and wellbeing in the work of the cross!

God wants to take your wounds, pain, hurts, and sorrow! Once again I'm reminded of the scripture from Psalms 40:11 & 12. It's about when David cried out to God; *"Now God, don't hold out on me, don't hold back your passion. Your love and truth are all that keeps me together. When troubles ganged up on me, a mob of sins past counting, I was so swamped by guilt I couldn't see my way clear. More guilt was in my heart than hair on my head, so heavy the guilt that my heart gave out."* (MSG).

Like David, maybe you feel the same way as you're turning the pages of this book. You may feel like trouble has ganged up on you. Maybe you feel swamped with guilt, shame and despair. But I'm here to encourage you. In Luke 12:7 the (NIV) Bible says, *"Indeed, the very hairs of your head are all numbered. Don't be afraid; you are worth more than many sparrows."*

Once again I remind you, there is nothing about you that is hidden from God. You have a God that knows the very number of the strands that are on your head! I love how the (NIV) Bible says in:

Psalms 33:13; *"From heaven the LORD looks down and sees all mankind;"*

Psalms 139:4; *"Before a word is on my tongue you, LORD, know it completely."*

Proverbs 5:21; *"For your ways are in full view of the LORD, and he examines all your paths."*

Jeremiah 23:24; *"Who can hide in secret places so that I cannot see them? Declares the LORD. Do not I fill heaven and earth?" Declares the LORD."*

Absolutely nothing about you is hidden from your God. Let's go back to the woman that was bent over for 18 years. God knew her situation; He was not surprised at her posture.

Before we move on any further, you have to come to the assurance that God wants to heal every area of your life. You must know you are significant to Christ and He has a perfect plan for your life. Absolutely nothing about you from the day you were born, to the very moment this book is in your hands, is hidden from God. He knows every single thing about you and, He loves you and died for you.

I love what Romans 8:38,39 (MSG) says; *"I'm absolutely convinced that nothing - nothing living or dead, angelic or demonic, today or tomorrow, high or low, thinkable or unthinkable - absolutely nothing can get between us and God's love."* Just for a moment, take a snapshot in your mind of a God that knows everything about you. The good the bad and the ugly and think about how scripture says He totally EMBRACES you! Wow. Let's just hang out in that thought for a moment and totally take in the embrace of our God.

Romans 8:1 reads; *"Therefore, there is now no condemnation for those who are in Christ Jesus."* (NIV). Jesus says with Him, there is no Condemnation. When you think of the word condemnation, it portrays an expression of strong disapproval, conviction, or judgment. When you are in Christ, you become brand new, your old ways are put behind you.

God's Word will begin to free you from the sins you have done. But the enemy is so clever and cunning. He desires to keep us in that place of guilt of our past failures and shortcomings, to make us feel we are beyond the reach of God's forgiveness. And, the devil wants to stop us from receiving God's forgiveness and make light of what Jesus did for us on Calvary. We can get in the way of receiving the freedom from condemnation. Remember, there is, *"No condemnation for those who are in Christ Jesus."* The price was paid when Jesus laid His life down on the cross for you and me, and He said, "IT IS FINISHED. PAID IN FULL." So with that being said, I decree and I declare, you are no longer bound; woman thou art loosed. It is time for you to hold your head up high, get back on your **Runway** and strut your stuff!

Will the real you please stand up!

No longer bound. I'm losed to be your devine design.

Confronting the Cover up

*C*onfronting the cover up in our lives is not always easy. But the beautiful thing is, you don't have to do it alone. Jesus said it best in John 16:7; *"Truly I tell you, it is for your good that I am going away. Unless I go away, the Advocate will not come to you; but if I go, I will send him to you."*

I love how through scripture we see we don't have to confront our issues alone. We have the Holy Spirit. The Holy Spirit is not an 'IT.' He is a person you can talk too. Jesus calls the Holy Spirit our Advocate. Unlike the Hollywood reports from tabloids, with their desire to sensationalize a person. The Holy Spirit will champion, uphold, support, promote, campaign, fight and crusade on our behalf. He is also a teacher. He will remind you of not just some things but everything. John 14:26 says; *"But the Advocate, the Holy Spirit, whom the Father will send in my name, will teach you all things and will remind you of everything I have said to you."*

In my process of confronting my cover up, I had to learn to be completely reliant on the Holy Spirit. Once we accept Jesus as our Savior and Lord, we become the dwelling Place of the Holy Spirit. 1 Corinthians 3:16,17 (MSG), puts it this way; *"You realize, don't you, that you are the temple of God, and God himself is present in you? No one will get by with vandalizing God's temple, you can be sure of that. God's temple is sacred—and you, remember, are the temple."*

Because the Holy Spirit lives in us, we have 24 hours, 7 days a week access to Him. Our access to him is ongoing. Giving us the ability to hear His Voice, know His will, thoughts, desires, goals, plans and vision for our lives, so we can accomplish all God has ordained for us to do.

Today I dare you to ask the Holy Spirit to reveal the areas you have been covering up. Ask him to help you see yourself as a victor and not a victim. Ask the Holy Spirit to reveal every hidden and secret thing so you can walk in the freedom God has ordained for you. Don't be afraid to ask the Holy Spirit to heal your broken and wounded areas that are hindering you from stepping onto your **Runway** as your authentic self. Why don't you take a moment to pause and write down what you sense the Holy Spirit is saying to you. Together, with the Holy Spirit's help and guidance, allow the healing to begin in you as you confront the cover up and step on your **Runway** of life.

I sense Holy Spirit is speaking to me in regards to:

_____
_____
_____
_____
_____
_____
_____
_____
_____
_____
_____

Will the real you please stand up?

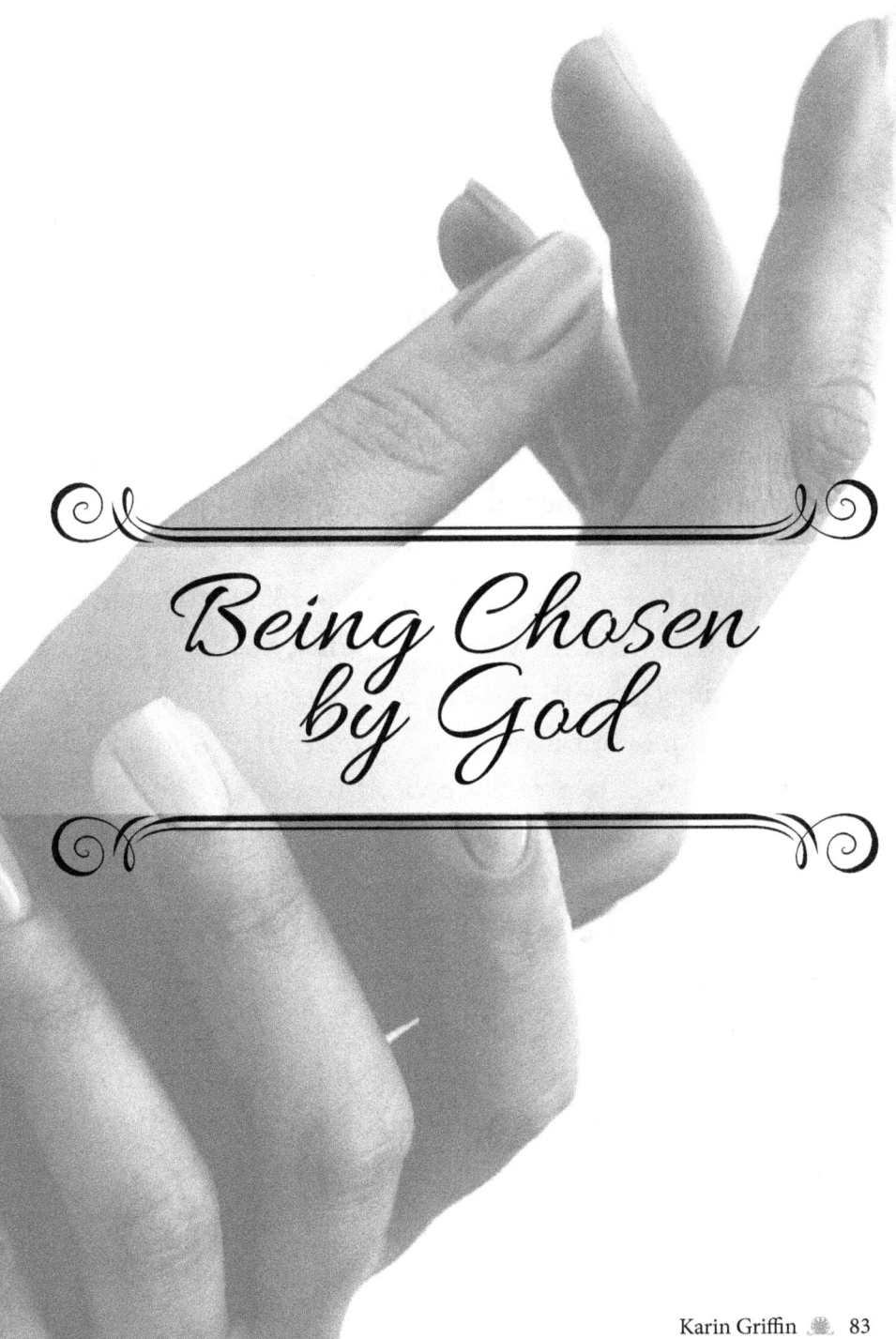

Being Chosen by God

Karin Griffin

Whether we realize it or not, we have been chosen, handpicked, preferred above others. Picked out, and given preference as God's elect person before we were ever born. (As I shared in the previous chapter when we spoke about the prophet Jeremiah.) Matthew chapter 22, verse 14 scripture says; *"For many are called, but few are chosen."*

So, as you can see, not only were we called by God to do great things as we daily walk this **Runway** of life. Living a victorious lifestyle with the freedom of using His Name in every situation of our lives. But, we were also handpicked, chosen and given a prophetic word through scripture to be fruitful and do great things in the power of His Name.

All year long the enemy is at work doing everything possible to cause us to stumble off of this **Runway** called life. He is constantly plotting and scheming, doing all he can to destroy our destiny assignments, wanting us to feel defeated, **NAKED** and spiritually stripped in the areas where we were created to flourish.

Maybe you're thinking, "Karin, I started the year out strong. I felt I could accomplish amazing things. I had great hopes and plans of overcoming obstacles, barriers, hurdles and things that have set me back for so long. But along the way I somehow became distracted, discouraged, bewildered, frustrated, fearful, annoyed, or defeated. I felt **NAKED** and I absolutely fell off course, feeling I could never accomplish all I desire to do. So I went back to what was my norm and covered up becoming totally numb while walking on my **Runway** of life."

My friend, I want to encourage you today to not give up; no matter where you find yourself, your story is not over! Get back up from your stopper and become committed and relentless to finish your course. Let me remind you again. You were handpicked, preferred above others and chosen by God to finish your race and finish-strong.

I learned long ago that EASY is not always part of the journey. It is sometime said; "The harder the battle, the sweeter the victory." As we walk this **Runway** of life, we will encounter spiritual warfare, but we have to remember we win!

John 16:33 tells us; *"These things I have spoken unto you, that in Me ye might have peace. In the world ye shall have tribulation: but be of good cheer; I have overcome the world."*

On this **Runway** we will have troubles. Tribulations will come, but be reminded God has overcome them all, and, trouble won't last always. I remind myself there is absolutely no trial, setback, failure or adversity I am not able to bounce back from. We just have to train ourselves to deal with our inner dealings and struggles. Taking captive any thought that is contrary to the goal, dream and desires that are so deep within our souls.

We also must know how to contend with our outer dealings and be very mindful and ever so careful whom we connect and share our plans and ourselves with. I've learned through the years that non-affirming relationships can hurt you and, set you back. You see by nature I am a people pleaser and desire to be liked. So I used to place a high premium on the thoughts and feelings of people close to me or people I looked up to or held in high esteem. And, if at any time they could not see what I saw, or see the value or worth in me, it would throw me off course. Without me even knowing it, I would go into a tailspin. Even now, reflecting on that has me exhausted. If you're by yourself in your room, just yell at me and say, "Karin what was your problem? You were giving them too much power!"

Yes I totally agree, too much power. You see non-affirming words or others opinions would allow me to fall off my **Runway**, right into someone else's lane. So I had to learn that someone else's opinion of me, about what I am setting out to do is not my problem. It's theirs. Often times there will be those who can't see what God is showing you and that's okay. Our job is to just stay focused and take responsibility for what we are called to do. So, with confidence, let's put on our 5-inch stilettos and get on our **Runway**; filling to the full our God given destiny!

> Scripture tells us in Ephesians 6:12: *"Our struggle is not against flesh and blood, but against the rulers, against the authorities, against the powers of this dark world and against spiritual forces of evil in the heavenly realms."* (NASB).

You see my friend; our fight is a spiritual fight. It is not against anyone in particular. It's about the enemy trying to steal our prophetic destiny we were birthed to fulfill. From the day we were born, the enemy has been studying, observing, watching, and looking for an avenue to sabotage our walk on the **Runway**. He will use whatever he can to cause us to miscarry our dreams, visions, desires, goals and aspirations; to destroy the, "Prophetic Word" God has placed on our lives.

> The word of God tells us in Revelation 12:10; "...that Satan accuses us daily before our Lord."

> Revelation 12 verse 10 reads; *"Then I heard a loud voice in heaven say: 'Now have come the salvation and the power and the kingdom of our God, and the authority of his Messiah. For the accuser of our brothers and sisters, who accuses them before our God day and night, has been hurled down.'"* (NIV).

The enemy is known as, "The accuser of the brethren." He's always accusing us, trying to make us feel we are not worthy to be **called or chosen** by a Great God. Think about it for a moment... In a very subtle but successful way, he persuaded Adam and Eve, that all that had been given to them was not enough.

Scripture tells us in Revelation 12:10; that satan accuses us to Jesus. But I say we must be uniquely aware; he also accuses and confronts us in our own minds. That is why it is so important we get rid of stinking thinking. Forfeiting and removing all the negative darts the enemy has thrown our way. Then we can see ourselves victorious on this **Runway** of life. Because of what Jesus did for us on Calvary, we have the ability to see ourselves as chosen, totally rejecting all the negative thoughts the enemy sends our way. We must be assured and confident what we have been given in Christ is enough. Through His promises, all the enemy's accusations and darts he tries to throw our way will not succeed.

We must be assured:
- **Satan is not our ruler.**
- **His accusations have no power.**
- **He cannot destroy us.**
- **He will not deceive us.**
- **Because our victory is in the shed blood of Jesus and what HE did for us on Calvary!**

I had to learn and I still practice daily to use the Word, as I confront my inner conversations and or dialog that I have with myself that are contrary to the will of God for my life. I also remind myself daily that I have been handpicked and chosen by God to do what no one else was created to do but Karin. So today, remember you have been chosen, handpicked, preferred above others, picked out, selected and given preference to do and birth out something no one else was **chosen** to do like you. So let's put on our spiritual stilettos, get back on the **Runway** and walk victoriously into our destiny finishing strong.

Will the real you please stand up?

I have been chosen to

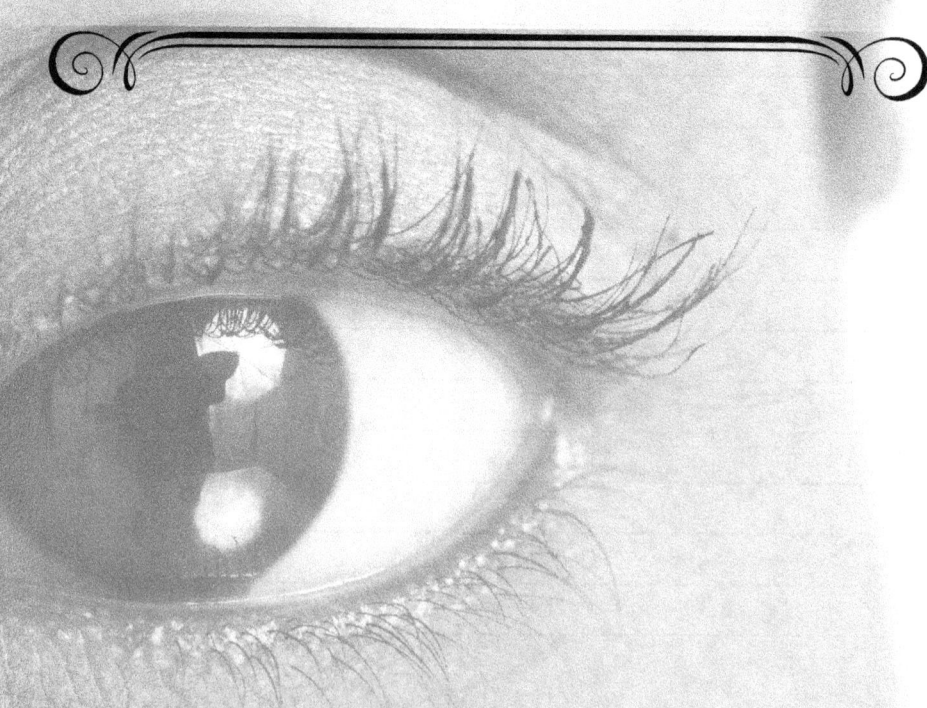

Who Am I?

As I do so many days on my **Runway** of life, I look in the mirror and ask, 'Who am I?' And, 'Who do people say that I am?' (Something Jesus Himself asked His disciples) in Mark 8:27-29: *"And Jesus went on with his disciples to the villages of Caesarea Philippi. And on the way he asked his disciples, 'Who do people say that I am?' And they told him, 'John the Baptist; and others say, Elijah; and others, one of the prophets.' And he asked them, 'But who do you say that I am?' Peter answered him, 'You are the Christ.'* (ESV).

And my answer to myself is usually, 'I'm a hairstylist, Pastor's wife, wife, mother and grandmother.' etc. and yet, like many of the well known actors, models and celebrities that walk the **Runway**, looking ever so gorgeous on the outside, something inside, so deep; longs for more. We know there is so much more than what meets the eye. Daily, as I visualize myself in my mirror, I know and feel, that I have not yet completely OWNED my zone!

I heard a well-known motivational speaker share one day about a woman that was very accomplished. She had a great career, family, children, finances everything in the natural that a woman could ask for. By every sense of the word you would have thought this woman had it going on. Yet, like so many of us that walk this **runway** daily, there was a longing on the inside that had not yet been fulfilled. Even those that were closest to her could not see her value or worth. Maybe had they known her value and worth, and encouraged her, their appreciation may have given her the courage to step outside of the box and completely OWN HER ZONE.

She was an educated woman with a Masters in Communication and she desired to be a motivational speaker. She had a special gift for words and would begin to write the most amazing poems that would have blessed so many, but sadly; because this woman never had the courage to raise her voice and take a stand allowing herself to become totally vulnerable and **NAKED** to possible slips, falls and bloopers on her **Runway** of life, she died before ever fulfilling her dreams.

Because we have been chosen, we have to be ever so determined to use everything in ourselves to free ourselves, and be our real self, the real you. My prayer is that as you read this chapter you will become **NAKED**, bare your soul and allow the real you to stand up.

> Philippians 3:12-14, (ESV) says; *"Not that I have already obtained this or am already perfect, but I press on to make it my own, because Christ Jesus has made me his own. Brothers, I do not consider that I have made it my own. But one thing I do: forgetting what lies behind and straining forward to what lies ahead, I press on toward the goal for the prize of the upward call of God in Christ Jesus."*

Like Paul, I have this knowing that there is more in me than where I am. Daily, I desire to press forward or strain forward towards the goal for the prize. We must wake up every day, determined to stay on this **Runway** of life. Challenging ourselves to be the person we were created to be, determined to, "Totally own our zones!"

Everyday we must see ourselves, through the eyes of Christ. We must courageously step outside of our comfort zone so that we can completely annihilate, obliterate and destroy every hindrance that would cause us to stumble, turn back, fall short and/or forfeit the very thing we were created to do.

Like the woman I shared about, one of the areas I have struggled with in the past, was my ability to see my worth. I struggled with feelings of inadequacy, which ultimately caused me to shrink down. If I can be **NAKED** and candid before you, I knew deep within the core of me, I could do it. I allowed my insecurities to cause me to masquerade because I knew darn well I had the resources by God's grace, knowledge, wisdom, to live out the dream He put within my soul. I had the ability to handle the business; If I would have only allowed the real me to stand up!

Maybe as you're reading this book, like me, at times you struggle and deal with negative thoughts. Thoughts of what others may be thinking about you. Thoughts you may even think about yourself, thoughts that would try to deter you, stop you and hinder you from fulfilling your walk on your **Runway**. I am reminded what the Word of God says in Philippians 4:8 (Aramaic Bible in Plain English; *"Therefore, my brethren, those things that are true, those that are honorable, those that are righteous, those things that are pure, those things that are precious, those things that are praiseworthy, deeds of glory and of praise, meditate on these things."*

Negative thoughts only come to cause you to not be in alignment with who you were created to be. They cause you to not step on the **Runway** that was created for you to STRUT down. The scripture that really gets in my business and gets me back on the path of being the true me that I was ordained to be is from Galatians 6:4 (NIV); *"Each one should test their own actions. Then they can take pride in themselves alone, without comparing themselves to someone else,"*

- I've had to learn to test and judge my own actions.
- I've had to learn to take pride and value my worth in what God has called **me** to do.
- I've had to learn to not compare myself with anyone else and, my goal is to run my race and stay in my lane, not allowing me to get out of alignment, forfeiting the **runway** I was ordained to strut down.

I'm almost embarrassed to say that I am still sometimes challenged with thoughts that are contrary to the will of God for my life, which causes feelings of insecurity, doubt and unworthiness to arise. I sometimes even find myself being concerned and overwhelmed with thoughts of what others, (my peers, my sphere of influence, my friends, my mentors, people I look up to), might think. I sometimes wonder what they would feel or think about me if they really, really, really, knew the magnitude of the dream that is embedded so deep within my soul. But immediately, once the Holy Spirit brings it to my awareness and, I allow the Word of God to bring me back to my true self, I challenge that negativity. I refuse to allow "MY" negative thoughts of what I feel the opinions of others may be about me or even my own negative self-talk about myself, to cause me to shrink down. I have come to realize those thoughts come to deter me from being the woman, the, "Complete Woman," I was ordained to be.

You see, revealing the real you is not always comfortable, it will take confidence. But I challenge you to find your voice, as I daily challenge myself. I've not always done it right, said it right or gotten it right, because it can be very uncomfortable allowing the real you to stand up, revealing your true self. It takes courage to become the person you know you were created to be. Voicing yourself, sharing and unveiling the true you can sometimes be difficult and intimidating. But, speaking out and expressing that you are determined to stand while owning your zone, and filling to the full the big goals, dreams and aspirations that have lain dormant for so long, is well worth it.

So daily we must be determined to stay aligned to the vision God has for us. The vision placed by His spirit, so deep within our heart and soul. We must forfeit every thought that is contrary to the visions that are so explosive deep within us, and that come alive when we dare to step on the **RUNWAY** that was uniquely designed just for us.

Before I conclude, let's go back to my original thought, "Who Am I?" Today I challenge you to ask yourself that. If you were to ask me, I can definitely without any question tell you who I am but I am also very careful of whom I share every dream, every vision and every desire with. But trust me, daily I challenge myself to get dressed, put on my spiritual stilettos and tell the real me, "Girl, it's time to stand up!"

Will the real you please stand up?

Who am I?

Slips and Falls

It takes courage and spiritual stamina to allow yourself to be exposed, unveiled and become completely **NAKED** as you dare to put on your 5-inch stilettos and take the spiritual journey down the **runway** that was divinely designed for you. Trust me, you will have slips and falls as the real you stands up. (Because she has laid dormant, hidden and unknown for so long, she'll have to gain her strength in her spiritual stilettos on the **runway**.) But in no time, if she stays focused; she will strut that **Runway** and own her zone.

As I have shared before, one of the struggles you have to be very aware and conscious of, is people. People that have had you in a box or can't see your worth, value or the bigger picture, will or may become uncomfortable with the authentic you. You may even become uncomfortable with the new you. But I double dog dare you, yet I triple dog dare you to set your face a flint!!!! Refuse to be moved or become distracted, and be ever so determined to finish your course; it's time to own your zone!

On this **Runway** I call "Life," I've learned that you will have slips and falls. During Fashion Week, designers have beautiful people walking the **Runway** in stilettos and platform shoes that have never been tested before, and often times the models will slip, trip or fall along the way. The one thing that never fails is their getting back up. They forfeit embarrassment, shame, laughter and even gasps coming from the seats of the on-lookers as they finish their walk. Like the models on the **Runway**, we will have bloopers, slips, and falls in life, but it's all part of us fulfilling the plan God has for us. I've come to learn and I always tell my children, "It's not how you start, but it's how you finish." As I shared in the previous chapter, we are a story being read daily as we strut down our **Runway**s. So we cannot allow the obstacles, barriers and hurdles in life to block us on our spiritual **Runway**. We are each a #1 N.Y. Times Best Seller; being read by people who are depending on us to finish our walk.

>Proverbs 24:16, (GWT) says; *"A righteous person may fall seven times, but he gets up again..."*

>Job 5:19, (NIV) tells us, *"from six calamities he will rescue you; in seven no harm will touch you."*

As you read this book today, you may be on your seventh fall, but God's Word promises, He will rescue you and no harm will touch you. We can never underestimate the Hand of God on our lives. Psalm 37:24, (NIV) says, *"Though we may stumble we will not fall, for the Lord upholds us in His hand."*

I am reminded of Elijah in scripture. After a long drought, God told him it would rain. Elijah took God at his Word, because he knew the Hand of God was on him, and, he prepared for rain. He told Ahab to go to Jezreel, because rain was coming. The beauty of this scripture is, because the Hand of God was upon Elijah, and he trusted the Word of God, Elijah was able to, on foot, outrun the chariots and horses of Ahab. In modern terms, on his spiritual **Runway** of life, Elijah was able to outrun, on foot, the fastest car known to man.

> 1 Kings 18:46, (AMP) we see; *"The <u>HAND</u> of the Lord was on Elijah. He girded up his loins and ran before Ahab to the entrance of Jezreel [nearly twenty miles]."*

When we hold onto the Word of God, trusting His Hand on our life, we will tap into, "A spiritual realm of acceleration," which causes us to defy any natural hurdle, barrier or obstacle. The rules will change in our favor, causing us to continue our strut in our spiritual stilettos on this **Runway** that I call Life.

I love a good book or movie that is full of suspense, laughter, tears and drama. A movie where the villain is defeated and the main character comes out on top. In II Corinthians 3:2 & 3, The (KGM) translation *Smile* (Karin Griffin Ministries) we are told we are living, breathing, walking letters being read daily. Whether you realize it or not, there are people depending on you to stay on the **Runway**. Conquering every fall, slip, trip or spiritual blooper. They believe you will have the courage to get up and put back on your spiritual stilettos and finish your strut on your **Runway**. Other people are given hope by reading the pages of your story. Believing if God's Hand is on you, giving you the victory, then He can do it for them as well. As you walk out your story, on-lookers are on the sidelines silently cheering you on and trusting you will rise up from every fall as the conqueror. Seeing your journey gives them the courage to rise up and start their process on their **Runway** of life.

Isn't it funny how the person who is the, "Top Model" today could very well not be the, "Top Model" tomorrow. No matter how hard they try, the standard for perfection according to the media and the world is so unattainable. It's amazing how often the very model that graced the **runway**s as if they had it all together, years later begin to bare their soul. They say, "If I could do it again, I would do it so differently." Or, "I would have allowed the real me to stand up." Sadly in life we don't have the opportunity to have a lot of do overs. Time seems to unapologetically fly by year in and year out. I can't even recall how often I have said, "There's not enough hours in the day!" Or; "Where did the time go?" What about, "Boy, how time does fly."

> Scripture says it best, in James 4:14; *"Why, you do not even know what will happen tomorrow. What is your life? You are a mist that appears for a little while and then vanishes."* (NIV).

So from a visual standpoint, our life is like an aerosol can of hairspray. Just imagine pointing the aerosol nozzle midair and as you press down, the mist comes out. We see it for a moment, and then POOF! It's gone. There

are three questions I often ask myself throughout the year, just to gauge if I'm on track. I review these questions so I won't look up one day and ask myself; "Where did the time go?"
- *Where have I been?*
- *Where am I at this moment?*
- *Where am I going?*

After asking myself those questions, I reflect on my dreams and goals that I set for myself. So often when I reflect back, I can honestly say I accomplished many things. But, in the core of me, I often know I could have done more. Oftentimes I find myself becoming restless, longing for something bigger and better. Because I am keenly aware my **DREAMS** and desires are not about me. Every vision, goal, **dream** and desire that is deeply embedded in my heart, is truly about the Kingdom Plan God ordained to be accomplished through me before I was ever born. I am reminded of a statement I read some time ago. "It's not as much about your vision, it's more about you being a servant of God's vision; carrying out a part of God's kingdom plan." Then the saying picks up at; "When you do life with God, God **dreams** life with you."

I don't know about you, but more than ever before; I desire for God to **dream** life with and through me. I love it! Thinking of this saying, removes all pressure off my shoulders. It makes me more aware, it's not me that comes up with the visions, **dreams** and desires, but it is God working through me. Placing great **dreams** within my heart.

So, let's go back to the thought, 'life is but a vapor,' and remember tomorrow is not promised. Although years have flown by, there are still great **dreams** that are burning within my heart. **Dreams** that keep me coming back year in and year out. **Dreams** I can't seem to ignore or let go. I am almost embarrassed to say this, but because I know I am CHOSEN, I will boldly say it. "The **dreams** that are so rich and alive in my heart are so vast and grand, it literally takes my breath away." Just the thought of me accomplishing the visions and **dreams** that are on the canvas of my imagination, is beyond anything I can comprehend to do on my own. I am once again uniquely aware I can only accomplish these **dreams** and goals with God's help and guidance.

Philippians 4:13 reminds me that I can do all things, not some things, but all things through Christ who gives me strength! I understand my destiny and reason for living, is driven by the **dreams** and desires that are so rich and alive in my heart. Time is valuable I absolutely cannot afford to have any wasted months, years, time, energy and space occupied with things that will NOT add value to my **dreams**.

So today I challenge you, if you've had a slip, fall or spiritual blooper get back up. You don't have time to waste. Tomorrow is not promised to anyone. There is a great work that only you can do, **dreams** that God wants to **dream** through you. He has an audience that is reading your story, and with every good storyline there are peaks and valleys. So whether you're at the peak or in the valley, don't forfeit the process, because every part of the process brings value to your storyline. Remember you are a #1 N.Y Times Best Seller.

Will the real you please stand up?

*Lord, strengthen me
to get up from*

Is Christ Enough?

My thought provoking question to you today is…**Is Christ enough?**

One day right in the middle of my devotion my heart was flooded with emotion as I began to sing a beautiful song by Hillsong United, titled, "Christ is enough." As I began to worship, my spirit was touched with the most amazing and thought-provoking question, "Karin, **am I enough?**"

Of course you know my immediate answer was, **"YES"** like…you are more than enough my Lord. And then as only the Holy Spirit could do, with a sweet and ever so loving and gentle voice, I heard again, "Karin, **am I enough?**" At that very moment a sense of conviction came over me and immediately I realized the Lord wanted to share something with me on my **runway called life**. So I listened.

I sensed He was saying, "At times I have not been enough for you Karin." Tears immediately began to stream down my face as I pondered on the many times throughout the years, I had lost faith and hope in the dreams God had placed ever so deep in my heart. I thought of how often throughout the years, I felt compelled and even challenged in my thoughts, to do things my own way. To get immediate results, outcomes and or satisfactions, instead of finding rest and faith in the promises of my God.

In that moment, I could not help but continue to ponder the ever so precious moments when I became impatient with His Process. Feeling as though God had forgotten me, exposed feelings of abandonment which enabled me from finishing my course. I vividly remembered moments and seasons where I found myself comparing myself with others. I Struggled with thoughts of insecurity, jealousy and competition. Feeling as though God cared about others and their desires more than me. I questioned if I had done something wrong, or had I sinned in any way to block, hinder or stagnate the very things I was trying to accomplish. Feeling this way only took me into a more vulnerable place of hiding and trying to fix it myself, instead of becoming **Naked** and vulnerable, trusting in God and the promises He had given me.

As the thoughts continued to flood my mind, once again, that same question filled my heart; "Karin, **am I enough?**"

As the tears continued to stream down my face, I very softly said to my God, **"I've not allowed you to be enough**." In that moment, I had to admit to myself that so often, on this **runway** I call life, I've allowed myself to get in the way and have not fully trusted the Lord to complete the work He has begun in me.

> PHILIPPIANS 1:6, (AMP) says; *"And I am convinced and sure of this very thing, that He Who began a good work in you will continue until the day of Jesus Christ [right up to the time of His return], developing [that good work] and perfecting and bringing it to full completion in you."*

Maybe today, as you're reading this book, you are thinking of areas in your life where you have not trusted Jesus to help you finish the work He has begun in you. Areas where you have aborted the process, where you have found yourself struggling with insecurity, jealousy and being competitive. Maybe you've struggled with feeling God has forgotten you. In the process, you may have made a decision to do things your own way instead of having faith in God. Possibly like me, you're saying today, "I have not allowed Christ to be enough for me."

Maybe you're reminded of times when it didn't work out the way you wanted. When you couldn't see clearly what was before you. When fear came in and gripped your heart. When things weren't adding up. When you were sick and tired of being sick and tired, and, you pushed Christ aside and took things into your own hands. Selah. [Ponder, think about it]... and, then say to yourself...**No, Christ has not been enough for me**.

I'm reminded in scripture, we don't have to depend on our strength. **Christ is more than enough**. Everything we need is in Him. And, we have to make a decision that no matter how difficult situations get, we're going to follow Jesus without turning back and trying to accomplish things in our own strength.

> Zechariah 4:6-7, KGM (Karin Griffin Ministries Translation puts it like this);
> "So he said to me, 'This is the word of the Lord to [Us]: 'Not by [our] might nor by [our] power, but by My Spirit,' Says the Lord Almighty. What are you, mighty mountain [Human Obstacles]? Before [us] you will become [flat]. [You will be destroyed! For our strength is in God.]'"

As you well know, on this **runway** of life, we will have challenges. We will have setbacks, struggles and situations that will come against us. But it's in those moments we must be secure and find rest in Christ Jesus. Realizing that **He is enough**; no matter what it looks like. We must REFUSE to allow ourselves to continue the process in our own strength.

Zechariah 4:6; (NLT); *"Then he said to me, 'This is what the LORD says to Zerubbabel: It is not by force nor by strength, but by my Spirit, says the LORD of Heaven's Armies.'"*

When we step out in our own strength, we are saying, **"Christ you are not enough for me**." We must never forget the God of Heaven's Armies, the God of angels armies, is ALWAYS by our side. **He is more than enough for us**.

The Holy Spirit took me to scripture in Habakkuk 2:4, where it tells us; *"Behold, his soul is puffed up; it is not upright within him, but the righteous shall live by his faith."* (ESV).
I was compelled to look at the verse in another translation, I went to the Amplified Version of Habakkuk 2:4,

look how it tells us here; *"Look at that man, bloated by self-importance full of himself but [his] soul [is] empty. But the person in right standing before God through loyal and steady believing is fully alive, really alive."*

I began to sense the Holy Spirit saying, "Karin, when I am not enough on the **runway** you call life, and you're no longer living **by faith**, your spirit will not be fully alive. And if you're not careful, pride will rise up. Trusting in your own abilities and strength, which will allow your soul to feel empty, bringing feelings of un-fulfillment. Causing you to grasp for anything within your own reach to bring fulfillment and satisfaction in those barren areas of your life." Selah...

As I meditated on the scripture I heard the Spirit of the Lord saying, "Karin I have amazing and wonderful things to accomplish through you and many others, so lives can be affected and changed. I want many to be set free and delivered from the strongholds that have held them down for so long. Allowing bodies to be healed, marriages restored and wayward children return to a place of safety and refuge. But so often the very ones I have chosen, who started on the right path, lose course. Because they begin to have faith in their own abilities, success, finances, education, fame, connections, victories etc. ... And, their faith is no longer in Me. I Am no longer enough, because their faith is in their abilities and their giftings I have so graciously blessed them with."

I went to Romans 11:29, (NIV) which tells us; *"For God's gifts and his call are irrevocable."*

Then I read, James 1:17, it shows, *"Every good and perfect gift is from above, coming down from the Father of the heavenly lights, who does not change like shifting shadows."* (NIV).

In that moment I felt a strong sense that our faith, my faith, your faith, should never be crossed or contaminated with anything other than our faith in The True and Living God, and what He did for me, for you, and and for others over 2000 years ago on that old rugged Cross on Calvary.

We cannot afford to allow our gifts, talents and treasures to come before our faith in The True and Living

God. Habakkuk made it very clear; there are those who were puffed up, and are depending on their own abilities. But truly in order for us to have a victorious lifestyle, we should always live by faith, knowing that Christ is enough.

Today, let's make a decision to get back on the **Runway I call Life**, and allow the God of angel armies, who is always on our side; to always be enough. I love watching **Runway** Shows. They always have the best music, which boosts confidence and gives mobility for every model to strut their stuff. Today, let's decide to put on our spiritual stilettos, get on our **Runway** and strut our stuff to the beautiful song by Hillsong United, declaring, professing, announcing with authority and conviction that, CHRIST is ENOUGH FOR ME!

Will the real you please stand up?

I trust you Lord to be enough in the area of

You are Enough

Did you know that you are enough? The one thing I struggled with in life, that kept me many days off of the **runway** of life was, I never felt I was enough. No matter how hard I tried to convince myself, my thoughts, and self talk would always emerge; haunting me with reasons why I was not enough.

One of the words I can remember so vividly in my mind, or should I say the phrase that I remember so strongly in my heart that was spoken to me on a number of occasions was, "You will never amount to anything." To me, that meant I was not enough! Those words sealed the deal right there! And, it drove the knife of doubt and sabotage deeper into my heart and soul. I can remember saying each time as I fought back tears after hearing those words, "See girl, you're not enough...you're not good enough." I can remember in my anger and or frustration, I would say, "I'll show you." But the words still lingered, and every time I fell short, didn't hit the mark, stumbled in my goals, made a mistake or didn't match up to others expectations; those words would haunt me over and over and over again.

Whoever said, "Sticks and stones will break my bones but words will never harm me." Did not know what they were really saying. They had no idea about the power, depth and magnitude of words. Words are powerful, words can be obstructive and destructive. Words can sabotage dreams, visions and goals if not used correctly. Words don't disappear into never, never land. Words linger long in the hearts of men and women, little boys and girls year in and year out. Damaging words causes us to forfeit and/or abandon the very thing we were created to do. These lingering words fuel negative feelings and thoughts like, "I'm not enough." Many people today are walking the **runway** haphazardly, struggling to stay the course because they refused to confront and acknowledge negative words that have been spoken over or to them. Unknowingly those words are still lingering and creeping up uninvited at very critical moments in our lives, with the goal of causing us to forfeit and or abandon our walk on the **runway** of life.

The enemy does not play fair. He knows if you ever confront the cover up and become **Naked**, baring your soul, exposing and confronting negative words, your walk on the **runway** will be exquisite, absolutely phenomenal. "On fleek," as my kids would say. The enemy's job is to rob us and set traps to sabotage our strut down the **runway**, which never gives us the freedom to see ourselves at our best.

> John 10:10, (NIV) makes it plain: *"The thief comes only to steal and kill and destroy; I have come that they may have life, and have it to the full."*

Gods purpose is for us to have an, "Over the top,"; "I'm going to show out!"; type of life. And that is what we should, 'Declare daily.'

Please don't get me wrong, my friend, I don't think the person that spoke negative words to me, purposefully meant those words to hurt me. I think those words were meant to challenge me so I would rise to the occasion. However the enemy used those words as a, 'jungle gym' on my heart and mind. Hearing those negative words caused me to jump from one area to another on the canvas of my imagination. Those negative words caused me to believe what was spoken over me so many times.

You see, I was never the prettiest, most likely you

succeed, the smartest, and, I lacked confidence. I wasn't funny. I was somewhat shy but, really the shyness was just masking insecurity issues. Now that I look back, I was a tad bit socially awkward and to top it off, I was the only child for the first 12 years of my life. I spent a lot of time alone, so I was always in my own head. I would take the negative words that were said to me and allow the enemy to wreak havoc in my mind and heart, causing me to believe the very negative words spoken to and about me.

In an earlier chapter I shared with you, *"As a man thinks in his heart so is he."* Proverbs 23:7. Boy, was my heart thinking I was not enough. As much as I wanted to share and become vulnerable expressing my emotions, feelings, thoughts and dreams, I refused to become **naked**. I was afraid to bare my soul. I just knew I would be the laughingstock to all that would hear what I had to say. In my mind, Karin just was not good enough!

I can't recall the second, minute, hour, day or year this scripture came alive to me, but when it did, it was like the old school candy, 'Pop Rocks' that exploded in my mouth. It went into my heart and took over my soul.

Philippians 2:5, (KJV) says; *"Let this mind be in you, which was also in Christ Jesus:"*

I realized I had to have the mind of Christ. I had to clothe myself with scriptures that validated me, and begin to see myself through the eyes of Christ; challenging myself to get back on my **Runway**. I began declaring that I am enough. Scriptures say when we are born again, we are made new through Him.

2 Corinthians 5:17, (NLT) says; *"This means that anyone who belongs to Christ has become a new person. The old life is gone; a new life has begun!"*

Let's just park on that scripture for a moment. 'You are new' and 'I am new.' In Christ Jesus; we have been given a fresh start, a new way of thinking and seeing ourselves. I love this quote that was shared with me some time ago. I'm not exactly sure where it originated from but it still resonates to me even to this day, and holds so true to my heart.

"Sometimes it's the people no one imagines anything of, who do the things that no one can imagine."

I'm reminded of a woman in scripture no one saw value in. The whole town was against her. She was labeled a divorcee, home-wrecker, woman of the streets, harlot, and the list goes on. She even had to go to the well to draw water when no one was around because, not one woman in her community wanted to deal with her, be seen with her or hang around her. They ostracized her on every turn. To top it off, her city was not a city anyone wanted to visit or found value in.

But despite all the naysayers, The Lord told his disciples, "I must go by the way of Samaria!" You see, He knew there was a woman there that had lost all hope in herself, and felt she was not enough. But our Savior saw value in her. He still had need of her and He wanted to help her get back on her **runway** of life. Allowing her freedom and liberty to live life again without anything distracting nor stoping her. Jesus went out of His way to clothe her in His Love and acceptance.

> John 4:7-9 states; *"A woman of Samaria came to draw water. Jesus said to her, 'Give Me a drink.' For His disciples had gone away into the city to buy food. The Samaritan woman therefore said to*

Him, 'How is it that You, being a Jew, ask a drink from me, a Samaritan woman?' For Jews have no dealings with Samaritans." (World English Bible).

This woman was astonished Jesus would even talk to her. She didn't think she had any value, not to mention Jesus would take time to speak with her. Funny thing, it wasn't an accident Jesus' trip to Samaria was very intentional.

John 4:3,4; tells us; *"He left Judea and departed again to Galilee. Now it was necessary that He go through Samaria."*

I don't know where you might be reading this book now, but, whatever city you're in and this book is in your hand; Jesus is visiting you. Letting you know you are valuable and that He loves you unconditionally!

As I daily meditated on this scripture it gave me life... I began to see my Worth, my Value, my Desires, and my Goals through Scripture. You see, this woman didn't have it all together. She had slept with different men, she had setbacks, she made mistakes. But the Lord took time to go out of His way to let her know, she was enough; just as you are enough.

> John 4:16-18 (NASB) tells us; *"Jesus said to her, Go, call your husband, and come here. The woman answered and said, I have no husband. Jesus said to her, You have well said, I have no husband, for you have had five husbands; and the one whom you now have is not your husband; in that you spoke truly.'"*

As you can see from the scripture above, Jesus was reading her mail. And, you know her mail did not look really good but, God had not given up on her. He still took time to stop in a city where everyone else would have taken the long route and not even passed through. But, He made a point to stop there; to meet this woman at the well in spite of what her situation and or circumstance was. Even Jesus' disciples were astonished he was taking time to talk to the Samaritan woman.

> John 4:27, shows us; *"And at this point His disciples came, and they marveled that He talked with a woman; yet no one said, "What do You seek?" or, "Why are You talking with her?"* (NASB).

Can you imagine the stares she received as the disciples came up seeing Jesus taking time out to talk to her? And yet Jesus made no excuses, He did not apologize. He continued His conversation with her because He knew she was a valuable girl and, she was enough. He had faith that this woman's past setbacks, shortcomings, insecurities, weaknesses, and her pedigree would not dictate her future.

I want you to know it doesn't matter what life looks like now, what people have said about you or think about you, what mistakes you've made, what side of the tracks you grew up on. God says you are enough; you are valuable.

I love how this woman's life was transformed in the presence of the Lord. She went from being a home-wrecker, a harlot, and the laughingstock of her community; to an absolute world changer that brought many people to know Jesus as the Ultimate Savior and Lord.

> John 4:28-30, (NASB) shows us, *"The woman then left her water-pot, went her way into the city, and said to the men, 'Come, see a Man who told me all things that I ever did. Could this be the Christ?' Then they went out of the city and came to Him."*

How amazing is this? Once this woman saw her value and her worth through the eyes of Christ, she was able to go back in the city with her head held high and share the good news of Jesus Christ. Letting them know; if He has forgiven me, and saw value in me, Jesus can do the same for you, and this little lady brought all those men to the feet of Jesus!

How glorious is that! What the enemy meant for bad in her life got turned around and caused a revival in the city of Samaria. And that was the day this woman realized; **she was enough**.

I don't know what words have been spoken over you or what mistakes you have made, what side of the tracks you grew up on. I decree and I declare; **today you are enough**. Time to get back on that **runway**, put on your spiritual stilettos and begin to strut your stuff once again and...

Will the real you please stand up?

The Lord has stopped by to tell me, "I am enough"

Power Dressing

Now because of all that is going on with social media, cell phones are readily assessable to expose all that takes place before one steps on the Red Carpet. It's amazing how we now have access to see the stretch limos lined up with different actresses, actors, models or socialites prepping as they exit the car. Often times we will see them take that last minute glance into the mirror making sure everything is on point. We are right there as their stylist touches up their hair and make up. We have even observed a seamstress stitching clothing at the last moment before they hit the Red Carpet; to ensure everything is fitting just right.

There's something about those moments, when you're able to peek in and see what's taking place behind the scenes. I don't look at it as though these people are arrogant, self-centered, conceited or into themselves. I look at it from a spiritual standpoint, and say, "They are POWER DRESSING!" They are confident and clothing themselves to make a grand entrance. Making sure everything is intact so they can walk and strut themselves down the Red Carpet making and leaving a powerful impression for all to see.

These people fascinate me because I look at them from a spiritual and prophetic standpoint. Amazed by their confidence and the painstaking time they take to Power Dress. Scriptures are so clear on how we should daily prepare ourselves to strut this **runway** of life. The scripture that empowers me to daily get up and dress myself for power, or should I say, to power dress, is in Romans 13:14; *"But be clothed with the Lord Jesus Christ, and do not listen to the flesh, to fulfill its desires."* (JB 2000).

NOW THAT'S WHAT I CALL POWER DRESSING!

When we listen to our flesh, allowing it's desires to speak louder than the Voice of God through Scriptures, the enemy will use our mind as a playground to see ourselves in a negative way. Instead of seeing ourselves through the Eyes of Christ. When you begin to meditate on scriptures and view yourself through the Eyes of Christ; the scripture will shine light on every negative thought that is contrary to the Will Of God concerning your life.

When you meditate daily on scripture, it will expose every negative thought. Wisdom will shine through scripture exposing thoughts that are not empowering or up lifting. We as Kingdom Minded people and children of The Most High God, must be very intentional and deliberate in our thoughts. We must allow the Word of God to strip us **Naked** of all negativity, so we can walk in wisdom from on high and not allow our thoughts that arise from the flesh; (our human weaknesses, insecurities and doubts) to be in control.

If we are not mindful and intentional, the flesh will have us looking crazy. Presenting ourselves as if we don't carry the goods to fulfill the Call God has placed upon our lives. My friend, we have been fully loaded with wisdom, knowledge and, The Mind of Christ to be champions, conquerors and absolutely fabulous on the **runway** we walk daily.

Philippians 2:5 tells us; *"Have this attitude in yourselves which was also in Christ Jesus,"* (NASB).

We must learn to challenge our irrational thought patterns with The Word of God. Because we have been empowered to fuel the vision God has placed in our heart. Just park on that thought for a moment...

God has given you everything you need on your **runway** to fuel the vision He has placed in your heart. Daily, when you get up, you have to Power Dress and renew your mind with The Word. When you apply The Word everyday, The Word builds confidence. When you have confidence through The Word of God, it gives you the ability to know you have everything you need to do what God has called you to do. As you apply The Word everyday, you will begin to strip yourself of all negative thoughts, and begin putting on The Mind of Christ.

> 2 Peter 1:3, (HCSB) tells us; *"His divine power has given us everything required for life and godliness through the knowledge of Him who called us by His own glory and goodness"*

Actresses, models and socialites take an extra moment to grab a last look before exiting their limousines, making sure they have everything in their possession to empower them with confidence. Having all they need helps them to Power Dress and; instructs them on how to strut their stuff! We have been given that same help, through the Power of the Holy Spirit. Scripture tells us in 2nd Peter 1 verse 3, that God, By His divine power, has given us everything that is required of us to do what He's called us to do.

Let's take a moment and think about those areas where we have not taken that last look. Let's look at those areas where we have just been getting on the **runway** sloppy, when we don't strip ourselves of things that are holding us back. Now just for a moment, let's begin to take those layers off. Let's take off the layers that no longer belong to us. How about the layer that no longer relates to you because you no longer see yourself by the flesh or follow its directives. Now do you see yourself through the eyes of Christ. Clothed and dressed in His wisdom?

I had to begin power dressing myself daily with positive affirmations and words that were spoken of me, and about me, through the eyes of Christ. Think about that. Every day when we get up, preparing ourselves for our day, we should dress for power! Not just the physical clothes, such as shoes, handbags, etc... We should not only adorn ourself with our outer appearance, but also spiritually we must power dress for success. Prior to us getting dressed, we must spiritually undress ourselves and become stripped **NAKED** from every negative under garment... Those secret and hidden things that have secretly lied to us through the years. Making us feel as though we are not good enough, not worthy enough, smart enough, faithful enough, wise enough, brilliant enough, to fulfill all God has ordained for us to do.

Daily we must remove all toxic people, voices, and influences from our space. This way, we can rid ourselves of everything and anything that would hinder us from taking off the frumpy, un-ironed, mix matched things that add no value to our lives. It is imperative and absolutely important we strip ourselves **NAKED** of all statements, accusations, negative words, stigmas, stinking thinking, labels, insecurities, sabotaging thoughts. Everything and anything that would hinder us from making our GLOBAL PRESENCE.

YES YOU HEARD ME, YOUR GLOBAL PRESENCE!

We were born to be global-minded people. We have been created in the image of God, to make a unique and mind blowing impact, with the intent on leaving our mark, completely owning our zone.

I'm reminded of a man in scripture who was determined to leave his mark and had a global mindset and view. Before I present the scripture to you, let me share a little bit about this man.

This man had a global mindset; he had dreams, upon dreams, upon dreams. He was full of visions, desires and aspirations The Holy Spirit revealed to him in his quiet moments, in the presence of the Lord.

One day this man decided to share his dreams with the people he felt would empower and encourage him to walk out the things that were burning so deep in his heart. But contrary to his beliefs, the very people he trusted and became vulnerable to; turned out to be dream killers or, as I shared in a previous chapter; Destiny Despisers.

So the dream killers or Destiny Despisers, begin to plot on how they could sabotage and kill his dream. Hey, do you realize we have a Destiny Despiser who is studying us; wanting to kill our dreams? I decree and declare today, as you hold this book in your hand, the Destiny Despiser has no authority over you. You will, "POWER DRESS." You will take off the grave clothes and the prison clothes CONCERNING YOUR DESTINY ASSIGNMENT. YOU WILL BECOME GLOBAL MINDED, and collide with Destiny on it's appointed day. Selah...

For the word of God says I can decree and declare a thing and it shall come to pass. So, see yourself fully clothed, suited and booted, dressed to the max; and on fleek; fulfilling the very purpose you were ordained to do.

Now let's get back to this young man. He shared his dreams, and those he trusted became jealous and envious. So, they plotted on how to take him down. What they did was put him in a pit, but the fear of God came upon them. They took the dreamer out of the pit and sold him into slavery.

So after being sold into slavery, he ended up in his slave master's house. But get this, God blessed him in his slave master's house. But sadly, while in his boss' house he was falsely accused and cast into prison.

I can just imagine, while in the Boss' house he thought, "This must be it. God is going to help me and my dreams are going to come to pass! I am going to be able to do everything God has called me to do." Then the enemy attacks him again. This time with a false accusation and this guy is put into prison and has to put on prison garments.

Wow, this man that had a dream burning so deep down inside of him was stolen from his fathers house, put into a pit, taken out of the pit, sold into slavery and ended up being blessed in his boss' house. Then, while at his boss' house he was falsely accused and put in prison. So he went from the pit to the palace then to prison…

Like this man; I don't care what you're going through. I don't care if you have had to put on prison clothes. Scripture tells us very clearly, as I've said before; God's Word is all-powerful. His Word is alive, it is applicable and relevant to every aspect of our lives. My spiritual mother has taught me never to read the Word of God as some dead history book. God's Word is alive and we can apply it and use it to breathe life into every dead situation concerning ourselves.

> Psalms 34:19, (NIV) tells us: *"The righteous person may have many troubles, but the LORD delivers him from them all;"*

Remember to, "Let this mind be in you that is also in Christ Jesus." What God has for you, God has for you and, no demon in hell can stop the plan! You might go through some things. Troubles may come, but I decree and I declare, as you hold this book in your hands; trouble will not last always.

So this man went from the pit after finding favor in the Boss' house, to being falsely accused and put into prison, placed in prison garments. But like this man, you have to know you are powerful and no matter where you go or where the Lord places you. Nothing is impossible for you to do.

No dream is so big we cannot accomplish it. No vision or task given us cannot be handled with The Word. God has given us everything we need to work across time zones, languages and cultures to deliver a successful outcome. This man was taken from everything that was familiar to him and sent to another country. When God has given you a dream, it does not matter what region you are located in, your dream will speak, and you will take off the prison clothes and power dress for success. Whether you are in the:

- U.S.
- Detroit
- Houston
- Los Angeles
- Miami
- New York
- San Francisco
- Washington D.C.
- Canada
- Calgary
- Québec City
- Toronto
- Vancouver
- Latin America
- Buenos Aires
- Guatemala City
- Mexico City
- Abu Dhabi
- Amsterdam
- Athens
- Barcelona
- Dubai
- Dusseldorf
- Frankfurt
- Istanbul
- Jeddah
- Johannesburg
- Kampala
- Kuwait City
- Lagos
- Stockholm
- Bangkok
- Gurgaon (New Delhi)
- Hong Kong
- Singapore
- Sydney
- Tokyo

You're probably saying, "Karin, what's the point in listing all of these places?" The Holy Spirit wants to say to you, "IT DOESN'T MATTER WHERE YOU ARE. I HAVE EMPOWERED YOU TO MAKE A DIFFERENCE! NO MAT-

TER WHERE YOU FIND YOURSELF. YOU MUST HAVE A GLOBAL MINDSET. IT'S TIME FOR YOU TO ALLOW YOUR GLOBAL PRESENCE TO BE KNOWN."

As I study the Word of God, one thing I've learned about this powerful unique and anointed man is, no matter where he went whether it was at his Boss' house or in prison; God's Hand was upon him and he prospered in those places. Maybe you don't see your location listed, it does not matter where you are. Just like the cameras in cell phones that creep in unannounced and are able to capture celebrities getting ready to walk the **runway**, The Holy Spirit wants you to know that His Eye is on you.

As I continued to study scripture, what I realized is; no matter where this man went, God's Hands, Eyes and Favor were upon him. Yes, he had many troubles, but our God is yet a deliverer.

While this man was imprisoned, God used him mightily and promoted him. One day this man encountered two people in the prison; a well-known Butler and the other a pastry maker, "Baker." They both had a dream that disturbed them. Because God's hand was upon this man in such a way, he was able to interpret the two very disturbing dreams. After receiving the interpretation, one guy died and the other ended up being released and was sent back into the boss's house. One day the boss had a dream. The Butler remembered what this young anointed man was able to do, because The Hand of God was on him. Let's just park for a moment. From a prophetic picture and standpoint, The Holy Spirit is saying to you now, "It does not matter your current location, destination or circumstance. God can still use you no matter how dark your current situation may seem. Your current situation is not your final destination. Selah...

If you haven't guessed already, the man who's story I am telling is Joseph. So let's get back to the story. Two long years later the boss (Pharaoh) had a dream. The butler proceeded to share with Pharaoh that while he was in prison, there was a young man that had a gift of interpreting dreams. Before I move on with the story, let's park for a moment so I can share something I learned from Joseph. Joseph was a man that refused to become bitter and volatile. While in prison he still allowed God to use him so others would be set free from the things that had them bound. Yet being bound and imprisoned himself, he refused to hold back his gifts. He continued to stay global minded and vision orientated. He was selfless and willing to serve others. Wow, that was a mouthful! Most of us would have become bitter, angry selfish, doubtful, full of hatred and disgusted. Instead of dressing for power, we would've been power-less; daily clothing ourselves with things that would only weigh us down.

> Take a look at Joseph with me in scripture. Genesis 41: 14 shows us; *"So Pharaoh sent for Joseph, and he was quickly brought from the dungeon. When he had shaved and changed his clothes, he came before Pharaoh."* (NIV).

What we will notice from a prophetic standpoint and picture is, immediately when the opportunity presented itself, Joseph shaved...meaning, ridding himself of everything and anything that might have attached itself to him from the inside growing on the outside. He refused to let the bondage and stigma of the pass go into the future with him. He immediately shaved it off. Joseph refused to present himself as a victim, carrying the baggage and weights that want to arise when opportunity presents itself.

What we also notice here through scripture, is Joseph immediately changed his clothes! Joseph may have been in prison physically but emotionally; I believe he was not. At the very moment I'm writing this book, my husband received a letter from an inmate in prison. This inmate is a man that is full of dreams, visions, aspirations and goals. One of the statements this man, or inmate said to my husband in the letter that absolutely blew my mind and, awakened my spirit was: "Pastor Fred, I am in a 6 X 7 foot cell and while I'm in the cell they may have control over my body, but not my mind. My spirit is free. And daily I'm thinking of ways of how I can be an asset to my mother, even behind bars." Scripture says, *"Who the Son sets free is free indeed."* So just like Joseph, this man's testimony is a beautiful picture of the life I believe Joseph lived while incarcerated.

We've often heard that action speaks louder than words. So Joseph's actions clearly shows us that he was prepared to meet opportunity when it arose from a mental standpoint. I can just imagine that daily on the canvas of his imagination, he envisioned the moment, second, minute, hour, day and year he would be set free. I can just imagine the picture he painted on that canvas of his imagination, was one where he would go dressed for success from a spiritual standpoint when the opportunity arose. He would rehearse over and over in his mind how he was going to quickly Power Dress and present himself when that day came!

I highly encourage you to go back and read the life of Joseph. Because I was only able to give you, "A birds eye view," from my interpretation. Sharing with you, how it has ministered to me. What I love about Joseph is that through all his ups and downs, twists and turns, pitfalls, valleys, highs and lows, he never gave up on his dream and at the end, his dream came to pass. Scripture says when it was all said and done; Joseph was second in command. Because Joseph kept a global mindset, he not only saved his family but he saved a whole nation of people.

Scripture clearly tells us that it is not about our outward adornment. But it's about what happens on the inside of our hearts that is important. Just imagine if Joseph had not kept a global mindset, had he not stayed focused on his dreams. Had he not been very intentional in all of his doings, while facing challenging situations. Joseph may have never been able to fulfill the dream and dreams God entrusted to him from his youth. Like Joseph, we must keep rational thought patterns. If Joseph had not kept rational thought patterns, his dreams would have been clouded and faded with all of the attacks that came his way as he walked his **runway** called life.

Joseph was a man that was determined to let, "The Mind of Christ," totally saturate him to the full. He allowed the mind of Christ to be in him that was also in Christ Jesus. Like Joseph, we must recognize that as children, men, women, boys and girls of the Kingdom; we will have afflictions. We will have setbacks but God will deliver us from them all!

Scripture says in Proverbs 23:7a, (NASB) ;
"For as he thinks within himself, so is he....."
I'll say it this way, ...'As a person thinks he is on the inside so is he.'

Like Joseph, in order for us to Power Dress, the dressing begins on the inside, then it will flow to the outside helping us to navigate this **runway** called life.

1 Peter 3:4, (NLT) tells us, *"You should clothe yourselves instead with the beauty that comes from within, the unfading beauty of a gentle and quiet spirit, which is so precious to God."*

Before we go any further, let's take a moment to sit back and take a deep breath. Let's take time to focus on areas in our lives where we may need to be touched up before we hit our **runway**. There may be areas that need to be stitched before we hit the Red Carpet. Maybe even areas where The Holy Spirit may need to shine His Light allowing us to have a spiritual makeover.

At this very moment, I don't know where you are right now in your walk on this **Runway**, I am not privy to the pit or prison that may have come your way. But what I do know and have learned is, when you refuse to allow the testing and trials of each day to cloud your vision, you, like the models, actors and socialites taking the time to take a last glance in your spiritual mirror will allow the

Holy Spirit to reveal how He wants to Power Dress you. Presenting you flawless, on this **runway** of life.

Will the real you please stand up?

I'm removing my prison clothes in the area of

*It's time for the real you
to please stand up!*

www.ingramcontent.com/pod-product-compliance
Lightning Source LLC
Chambersburg PA
CBHW050554300426
44112CB00013B/1906